EXPLORING WRITING
IN THE
CONTENT AREAS

Teaching and Supporting Learners in Any Subject

Maria Carty

Pembroke Publishers Limited

© **2005 Pembroke Publishers**
538 Hood Road
Markham, Ontario, Canada L3R 3K9
www.pembrokepublishers.com

Distributed in the U.S. by Stenhouse Publishers
480 Congress Street
Portland, ME 04101-3400
www.stenhouse.com

We acknowledge the financial support of the Government of Canada through the Book Publishing Industry Development Program (BPIDP) for our publishing activities.

We acknowledge the support of the Government of Ontario through the Ontario Media Development Corporation Book Fund.

Library and Archives Canada Cataloguing in Publication

Carty, Maria

   Exploring writing in the content areas : teaching and supporting learners in any subject / Maria Carty.

Includes index.

ISBN 1-55138-188-5

   1. English language—Composition and exercises—Study and teaching (Elementary) 2. English language—Composition and exercises—Study and teaching (Secondary) 3. Language arts—Correlation with content subjects. I. Title.

LB1631.C445 2005   808'.042'071   C2005-903722-9

Editor: Kat Mototsune
Cover Design: John Zehethofer
Typesetting: JayTee Graphics

Printed and bound in Canada
9 8 7 6 5 4 3 2 1

Contents

Preface

Writing beyond the English class is a reality for adolescent learners. Students of science, social studies, mathematics, and health are frequently required to demonstrate their understanding of concepts through writing. How, then, can teachers of these subjects support students and assist them in creating quality representations of their understanding, especially as they may have little background in content-area writing?

When something is new and unfamilliar, we explore it. When we want to know more about a topic, we read about it, talk about it, think about it, test it. Scientists explore the oceans, the land, outer space. Social scientists explore cultures, history, our world. Health professionals explore the human body, the world of medicine, physical fitness. Mathematicians explore the world of data, numbers, relationships, statistics. This book is designed to help teachers of these very subjects explore what it means to write in the content-area classroom, to help them see where writing fits in their classrooms and in the lives of their students. It provides some background information about writing as well as a collection of practical ideas that teachers can use to support students in any subject area. Part 1 deals with the processes involved in writing, including suggestions for everything from generation of ideas, to drafting, to editing, to presentation. Following this is Part 2, which addresses the purposes of text, takes a closer look at a number of text frames and gives suggestions for creating each type of writing. Finally, Part 3 looks at assessment or providing feedback to students about their writing.

In addition to the practical strategies and ideas, each section includes a Word Wise, in which key words are listed. These are words important to understanding that aspect of writing and/or words that may be unfamiliar to students. Many sections include an Across the Curriculum text box that provides suggestions and ideas for using the activity across a variety of subject areas.

Some of the ideas in this book can and will be used repeatedly. Others are instructional ideas that may be necessary only once, as a means of introducing a topic or kind of writing. Certainly some may not be necessary for you and your students at all. There are other sections of this resource that can and will be used solely for reference. Deciding what to do and when to do it is only part of the responsibility of a teacher, and these decisions can only be made by the person who knows the students and their needs —you.

PART 1

Processes Involved in Writing

Most teachers and students are very familiar with the writing process: a series of steps or stages that a writer goes through in crafting his/her piece. This writing process is often described in a linear or cyclical fashion, where a student must think and brainstorm before he/she can move on to drafting, and then follow with revision, then editing, and finally publishing.

In this part you will find key words, practical strategies, and ideas organized around innovative ways to incorporate the writing process or processes into your classroom instruction.

Process or Processes?
Possibilities: Brainstorming and Generating Ideas
Putting it in Your Own Words: Research and Note Making
Paragraphing: Organizing and Drafting
Presentation and Conventions: What Counts, What Doesn't
Pictures, Charts, Graphs, and Other Visuals: Supporting and Extending Learning

Process or Processes?

Word Wise

process
researching
note making
organizing
drafting
reviewing
revising
editing

There are specific processes that every successful writer engages in along his/her journey in writing; however, it is important to recognize that each writer approaches the task of writing in a different way. It is unrealistic to expect that every student's writing will progress through the same steps in a common sequence. This difference in the process is very much linked to purpose (the reasons for the writing) and audience (who the writing will be shared with). Writing that is to be shared and/or evaluated by others is much more likely to be worked through more processes or steps in an effort to ensure that it is clear, accurate, and positively received.

The following graphic illustrates some of the processes that are involved in writing, highlighting the interconnected nature of writing. Presenting these processes as a web makes clear that not all writing will involve every one of the processes mentioned, and that a writer may engage in these processes in any order. Some writers begin with thinking about the topic and organizing their ideas; others begin writing, and think and organize as they go. The use of technology, such as word processing, has and will continue to have a great impact on the way people write. Writing on a computer may mean that organizing, drafting, revising, and editing all occur simultaneously.

Across the Curriculum

As a writer of nonfiction, think of the last piece of writing that you completed. Using the visual provided, try to trace the process you engaged in as you were writing. No doubt you will find that your process was not a simple one, nor unidirectional. If you were to compare your process to another person's, you would likely find that you each took a different route.

Ask students to use a colored marker to trace the process they used when writing a piece of text. Then ask them to compare their web with those of three or four other people. These webs will give students a visual that represents the complexities and individuality involved in writing.

Processes of Writing

Understanding that there are multiple processes is not enough. It is also important to remember that students need support and instruction in how to successfully engage in each of these writing processes. We can't assume that all students know how to effectively make notes or research a topic. Explicit instruction in these areas is a small investment that can pay off in the long run.

Part of the investment means making sure that both teacher and students understand the processes involved in writing. The processes are introduced here; more detailed suggestions regarding how to engage students in these processes can be found in the following pages.

 Thinking and Generating Ideas

This is when the writer considers both his/her interest and expertise, and determines what to write about. It is also the process of generating ideas for a piece of writing, either assigned or selected. Ideas are not only those specific to the content or the information that the writer wishes to convey, but also include those about how he/she will convey this message through writing.

 Researching and Gathering Information

This is the collection stage. Information can be gathered from a variety of sources— personal knowledge and experience, talking with others, or reading and viewing related texts.

 Note Making

As a part of the writing process, note making requires the student as writer to record ideas and information in a form that can be useful later. It is important that these notes be accurate, and written by the student for the student. In other words, they need to be written in the student's own words, not simply lifted from the text. During this part of the process, meaning-making is also occurring, and it is this meaning that the student will try to convey through his/her piece.

 Organizing

Organizing involves the writer in making decisions about the structure of the piece. This includes identifying main ideas, determining a framework, grouping similar ideas, and sequencing this information. This is all about the writer determining the flow and deciding how best to achieve his/her purpose.

 Drafting

The writer gets ideas on paper and begins to develop the piece. During this part of the process, a lot of information may be recorded that may be changed or eliminated at a later stage.

 Reviewing and Revising

This involves reading the written draft and making decisions about what to keep, change, or eliminate. The emphasis at this point is on improving the substance of the piece. Revising requires the writer to look at the meaning that has been recorded and to try to ensure that what has been written achieves his/her purpose for writing.

Editing and Polishing

Editing is the process of making smaller changes or fine tuning the text in order to produce a piece of writing that achieves its purpose and is ready to share with others. This may include correcting spelling, punctuation, use of capital letters, grammar, paragraphing, and sentence structure. At this time writers may also improve word choice.

Presenting and Sharing

This is the process of creating the final piece and making it available to others. Many writers choose to present their work in final copies that have been created on a word processor, that incorporate visuals and color, and that represent their best efforts. Final copies may also include work that has been written by hand. The options for sharing include reading orally to or with others, allowing other students to read from the print copy, or simply giving a copy for the teacher or others to read in private.

Across the Curriculum

As a content-area teacher you may find that some parts of the process have greater appeal and relevance than others. Thinking, researching, note making, and organizing ideas are essential aspects in developing a greater understanding of any concept. It is important that the communication side of things also be reinforced. The processes of drafting, reviewing and revising, editing and polishing, and presenting and sharing all have impact on the end result.

Because time is an issue, consider short mini lessons. Or try teaming up with the English teacher, who can do some of the initial instruction while you can provide reinforcement and follow up. One of the most important things that content and English teachers can do is to discuss, agree upon, and reinforce a set of common expectations for written work. Common expectations may include

- decisions about use of paper: use both sides or one side, lined or plain paper, single- or double-spaced, printing or handwriting, etc.
- a common set of editor's marks
- use of conventional spelling (when is it required? not required?)
- use of conventional punctuation (when is it required? not required?)
- use of capital letters (when required? not required?)
- use of conventional grammar (when is it required? not required?)
- format for note making
- format for title pages
- format for citing sources
- format for bibliography
- expectations for constructing visuals: maps, graphs, charts, diagrams, etc.
- use of common assessment rubrics for nonfiction writing

Possibilities: Brainstorming and Generating Ideas

Word Wise

graphic organizer
web
flow chart
Venn diagram

For some students, the hardest part of writing is deciding what to write about. This might involve choosing a topic; if the topic is already determined, the student may still be unsure what to include in the writing. The activities below offer some suggestions for helping students get ideas down on paper.

Ask students to keep an ongoing list of topics they could write about. This list can include topics of interest, topics about which the student has some knowledge or expertise, topics assigned by the teacher, etc. It is possible to narrow the topic list by having students create possibility lists for specific units of study.

See Possibilities List (page 81).

Across the Curriculum

In a Grade 8 math class, students are asked to create a possibility list for a geometry unit:

Pythagoras: who was he?
How does the Pythagorean relationship work?
Everyday uses and application of Pythagorean relationship
Why the Pythagorean relationship was an important discovery
What I think the Pythagorean relationship represents

Graphic Organizer: Word Web

When a topic has been identified, a basic word web can be used to brainstorm what the student already knows about the topic. In the centre of the web, the student records the topic. Radiating out from the centre is the information the student wants to hold for future reference.

If more detail and organization are required, students may choose to use a cluster web. Again, the student records the topic in the centre. Similar details are grouped together and recorded on the outermost part, or third layer, of the web. The second or middle layer of the web can be used to record subcategories of the main topic. These subcategories should accurately describe the details that are attached.

See Basic Web (page 82) and Cluster Web (page 83).

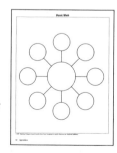
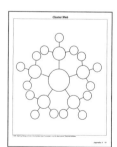

Other Graphic Organizers

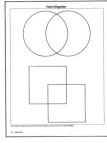

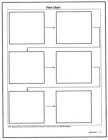

See Venn Diagrams (page 84) and Flow Chart (page 85).

While a word web is a graphic organizer, it provides little structure. If a more detailed framework is required for recording information about a topic, students can use—or better yet, can create—more sophisticated graphic organizers.

Graphic organizers have long been promoted as a tool to support reading and comprehension. The advantages of a graphic organizer to support writing are numerous as well. For the student who is unsure what to include in their writing, the graphic organizer provides some direction. Each section prompts the students to include a particular kind of information.

All graphic organizers are not created equal. The effectiveness of a graphic organizer is dependent on its fit with the purpose for writing. For example, a flow chart is often used prior to creating procedural or sequential text, whereas a Venn diagram can assist in creating comparative text; the two cannot be used interchangeably. Another common and very flexible graphic organizer is the three-column chart. This frame works well for both persuasive text and personal response, provided the headings or prompts are appropriately selected. For more information about text patterns see Part 2: Purposes of Writing.

Idea Sketching

It is important to remember the value of visual forms of representation even in the early stages of writing. For some students, the opportunity to record initial ideas through pictures and not words can be very helpful. In idea sketching, students record their ideas for the writing first in visual form. A single sketch could record a singular idea; a series of sketches, similar to a storyboard, could be used if the writing is about a process or a series of events. Once the student has the picture of what he/she wants to write about, he/she can begin to put this into words, describing the most important aspects of the picture in his/her written explanation.

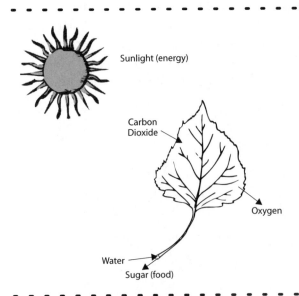

Plants need water, energy (sunlight), and carbon dioxide in order to make food (sugar) to grow. The process is known as photosynthesis. When photosynthesis happens, oxygen is also given off by the plant. This helps the environment.

Putting It in Your Own Words: Research and Note Making

<table>
<tr><td>

Word Wise

note making
note taking
source

</td><td>

It is important that students learn how to gather information from other sources and record it in a way that is meaningful and represents personal understanding. Too often students will record word-for-word what appears in the original text, without any attempt to synthesize it with prior knowledge.

</td></tr>
</table>

Note making and note taking are two terms that are sometimes used interchangeably. For the purposes of this book the following definitions will be used:

- **Note making** involves the student in reading, listening, or viewing new information, synthesizing it, and then recording important information in a manner that can be useful at a later date.
- **Note taking** includes writing notes that are provided by the teacher. Student may copy notes from the board, or overhead or LCD projector.

Because note making requires a higher level of thinking and processing, it is something that needs to be explicitly taught to students. Many show up in middle school or junior high and are at a loss when it comes to note making. A simple approach to teaching adolescents how to make notes includes three kinds of instruction.

- Direct: model and demonstrate how to make notes.
- Supported: using an overhead or LCD projector, work with students to make notes as a collaborative activity.
- Independent: provide opportunity for practice and purposeful application.

In addition to having a process for instruction it is also helpful if students have a framework for note making. It is especially helpful if this framework is common to all subject areas. The use of a common framework by students is the payoff for the up-front investment of teaching students how to make notes. When students have more opportunities to use the framework, their comfort level, skill level, and quality of work will increase. Here are three different note-making frameworks.

Note-Making Chart and List

See Note-Making Chart (page 86).

A chart provides students with a number of options. If a high level of support is required, teachers may choose to provide the key vocabulary prior to the lesson, allowing students to establish a context, ensuring correct spelling of key terms, and giving students an indication of what information should be included in the important information section. Once students have recorded important information in the centre, they can go back to the outer columns. Students should record a summary sentence(s) that sums up the information in the centre. Students can also include a visual (diagram, graph, chart, etc.) to support the information recorded, and record questions that they still have.

See Note-Making List (page 87).

The outline format for note making is the traditional approach. Notes are made in a hierarchical manner. Information is presented levels, and a series of numerals and letters is used to organize the it: the topic or title is recorded across the top; subheadings are indicated by numerals; sub-subheadings are arranged by lower-case letters below sub-headings; details are arranged by roman numerals below subheads.

What/Did/But/Result (WDBR)

See WDBR (page 88).

The What/Did/But/Result provides a framework for students to locate and examine the key elements in information text. After reading, the student writes a single sentence in each of the boxes.

- In the What box, the student writes a sentence explaining what (or who) the text is about. If he/she is reading in science about erosion by water, the student could write, "Water causes erosion."
- The Did box is where the student would write the action. He/she may write, "Waves pound against the shore, and rivers run through the land."
- The But box is the place to note any conditions or factors that affected the action. Here the student may say, "Erosion happens quickly when the soil is loose, but takes thousand of years if rocks are big and hard."
- In the Result box, the student records the result of the action. In this case the student could write, "The force of pounding waves, and running water eventually wears down and washes away even the hardest land."

Once the student has filled in each of the boxes, he/she can then try to create a single summary sentence using the information. A summary sentence for the above example might be, "Erosion caused by water happens when waves or rivers move over soil and rock causing it to break down into smaller pieces and eventually wash away."

Quotes vs Copying

A direct quote is something that is lifted from the text and recorded word-for-word. It is important that use of direct quotes be signaled by quotation marks, and that a reference is made to the source, where the quote came from. When the author's exact words are not used, but the author's ideas are, it is important that students know how to cite or reference the source in order to give the author credit for his/her ideas and work. (See pages 22–23 for information on citing sources.) Students should be encouraged to use quotation marks and to document sources in their earliest notes, reducing the opportunity to forget where the information came from and which parts of the notes are direct quotes.

Paragraphing: Organizing and Drafting

Word Wise
paragraph
artifact

Paragraphing is an important writing skill that many students either have forgotten or never really learned. The reality is that most, if not all, students will have been taught about paragraphs in elementary school, but some will continue to need support when it comes to organizing their writing into paragraph form. These easy activities will help students to "see" paragraphs and incorporate them into their writing.

"Who Am I?" Artifacts

This is a great activity to do at the beginning of the year as people get to know each other.

1. Bring a collection of artifacts to school to share with students. This collection should include things that tell something about you as a person. When I did this activity, my artifacts included photos of my family, my wedding invitation, a business card, my résumé, my travel journal and photos from a European vacation, a favorite book, a pair of snowshoes, etc. Essentially, anything counts.
2. Share each of the artifacts with the students and ask them to discuss what they can tell about you as a person from examining the artifact.
3. Each student should choose one item and record on an index card observations and questions.
4. Ask students to gather in groups. Those who have similar items should form a group. Each group must identify themselves based on topic. It is likely that there will be groups representing family, hobbies, work, etc.
5. Each group collaboratively writes a paragraph describing one aspect of your life. Groups should be reminded to include an effective topic sentence based on their group identity and to ensure that each artifact has two or three sentences dedicated to its description or discussion.

Across the Curriculum

The Artifacts activity can be adapted to suit a science or math class. Instead of sharing personal artifacts, share artifacts that are specific to the subject area. For example a Math Tools collection might include a calculator, a compass, a protractor, an abacus, a number line, a ruler, counters, etc. Students can then discuss which items they consider to be similar in terms of their use or function. They may decide that the calculator, abacus, number line, and counters can all be used for computation—to add, subtract, multiply, and divide. The group can write a paragraph about the tools of computation.

From Sticky Notes to Paragraphs

1. Have a student read aloud a piece of writing that lacks organization and paragraphing.
2. As the student reads, quickly record on small sticky notes the general topics or ideas that are mentioned. For example, as a student reads you might record the following

things: has 1 brother, enjoys English and Phys Ed, favorite food is pizza, favorite TV show is *The Amazing Race*, best friends are Robin and Tam, dislikes science, plays hockey and basketball, dislikes green vegetables, etc.

3. Share the sticky notes in the order they were recorded. It is easy to see that such a list lacks organization.
4. Have the student group ideas together.
5. When the student revises the piece, each sticky note represents at least one sentence. Each group of notes is a paragraph.

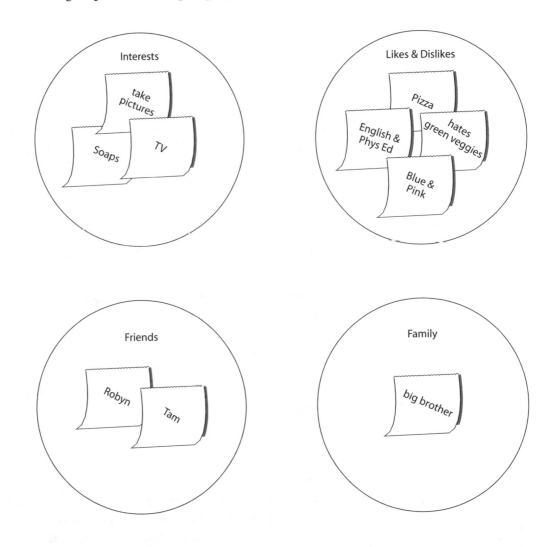

TIPS for Beginning New Paragraphs

A new paragraph is need anytime there is a change in one of the following areas:

- **Time:** hours, days, months, etc. have passed
- **Ideas:** a new idea/topic/concept is introduced
- **Place:** the location of the story has changed
- **Speaker:** in dialogue between characters, a new person is talking

Presentation and Conventions: What Counts, What Doesn't

Word Wise

presentation
conventions
spelling
punctuation
grammar
sentence structure
references
bibliography
title page

In some cases, the substance of a student's writing is strong, but the piece is poorly presented. When this happens, there is opportunity for miscommunication and misunderstanding. As well, writing that is filled with spelling, grammar, and punctuation errors is often difficult to read and its strengths are overlooked. This section provides some basic information on presentation and conventions. While content-area teachers may not have the primary responsibility for explicitly teaching the rules of presentation, the information presented here can be useful in developing a common language, as well as common understanding and expectations, in order to provide students with consistent feedback about their writing.

Across the Curriculum

This section is a good place to begin the consultation process with other teachers in the school. When expectations are consistent across the grade level, both the student and teacher have greater opportunity for satisfaction.

Format Options

The decision about how to format/design/present writing is all about aiming for readability. There are many things that will enhance readability, and many that will detract from readability. The list below offers a few suggestions for students to consider when planning the presentation of their work.

Watch your margins and spacing.

- leave a margin around all sides of your page
- use a standard font of 10 to 12 for standard text, larger for titles and subtitles or for effect
- when printing or handwriting, keep the letters within the lines and evenly spaced
- use single spacing unless extra space is needed.

Use headings for longer pieces of writing.

- keep headings brief
- use the same style for headings of the same level

Consider using lists.

- use bullets if the list is in random order
- use a numbered list if there is a sequence or an order of importance to the list

Consider including visuals.

- include visuals if they support the text
- include visuals to extend or go beyond the information presented in the text

Consider using color.

- use color to draw attention to headings and subheadings
- use color for visuals, such as graphs, maps, diagrams, etc.
- colored borders can add visual appeal

Style: Spelling

See Top-Ten Spelling Strategies (page 89).

There are times when spelling counts and students are expected to use conventional spelling in their writing. This is particularly challenging when you think of the content areas and the amount of technical vocabulary that students are required to use in their writing. How can we help students without doing all the work for them?

Teach students how to use the tools available to them.

The best source for finding the correct spelling of technical vocabulary is the textbook. Key places to look for technical vocabulary include

- bold print
- headings and subheadings
- in captions
- as part of graphs, tables, charts, diagrams ,etc.
- in the glossary

Also teach students how to use a dictionary and try to have copies of a dictionary specific to your subject area handy for them to use. Many general dictionaries may not have some of the words they need.

Create word banks or word lists.

For each unit that you teach, keep a bank of common and important words on a chart or poster that the class can keep updated. This should be posted in a prominent place in the room so students can refer to it as necessary. Students should understand that it is expected that these words be spelled correctly in their writing all the time.

Style: Punctuation

See Basic Punctuation chart (page 90).

Writers use punctuation within and at the end of sentences to help the reader understand what the author has to say. It is important to decide for and with students what the basic expectations are for correct usage of punctuation. This strategy is most effective if the expectations remain the same in all subject areas. In the case of younger students, the expectation may be that students consistently use end punctuation correctly while they work toward or develop their use of other kinds of punctuation. Older students may have similar expectations for correct usage of end punctuation, but also be expected to consistently use quotation marks, the apostrophe, the colon, and the comma; punctuation like the semicolon may fit in the developing category.

It is also important to discuss the importance of using standard punctuation in work that is going to be shared with others. For work that is personal (e.g., note making) it may be less of an issue; there needs to be enough punctuation that the student can later read and understand what has been written, but perfection may not be required.

Style: Sentence Structure

Sentence structure includes how you organize the parts of your sentence. Effective writing uses a variety of sentence structures in order to make the writing clear and more interesting. Here are some tips for effective sentence structure:

- Use sentences of varying lengths: some short and some longer.
- Vary the way sentences begin: don't being with the same word/name more than two times in a row.
- Include questions and exclamations as well as statements, using appropriate punctuation.

Type of Sentence	Example
Simple sentence: contains one main clause	Canada is a large country.
Compound sentence: contains two or more main clauses joined by a comma and/or a coordinating conjunction (*and, or, for, but, so, yet*, etc.)	e.g., Canada has ten distinct provinces and three territories, yet its population is relatively small.
Complex sentence: Contains a main clause that can stand alone as a sentence, and one or more subordinate clauses.	Canada, one of the world's largest countries, has a total area of 9 984 670 km^2.

When helping students revise their writing, a few practical suggestions can help them create writing that effectively communicates their ideas.

Use a combination of simple, compound, and complex sentences.

If your writing often uses a series of simple sentences, try combining sentences.

> The world has 7 continents. Asia is the largest continent.
> The world has 7 continents of which Asia is the largest.

Don't assume better writing consists of a series of long sentences.

Use some short and some long sentences to make writing more interesting.

> The United States of America declared its independence in 1776 . Originally a country consisting of 13 states and a small population, it has grown to a population today of 296,000,000 people living in 50 states.

Vary the way you begin sentences.

A report in which most sentences begin with the subject of the report is not engaging. Don't repeat the same lead more than twice in a row.

Try "flipping" sentences.

Reverse the information at the beginning and end of the sentence.

> Sir Sandford Fleming invented the concept of time zones and standard time.
> Time zones and standard time were invented by Sir Sanford Fleming.

Style: Grammar

The following reminders will help students eliminate or at least reduce the most common instances of poor grammar.

Avoid fragments.

Fragments are incomplete thoughts. Make sure every sentence has a subject (who or what the sentence is about) and a verb (action word).

> In math class I sat in my usual seat, the third seat in the second row.
>
> **not**
>
> In math class I sat in my usual seat. Third seat in the second row.

Avoid run-on sentences.

A run-on sentence has more than one main idea, and ideas are not connected grammatically. Break into smaller sentences, or use a comma or conjunction to fix.

> In schools fights can occur and students feel unsafe. What purpose does this serve?
>
> **not**
>
> In schools fights can occur and students feel unsafe, what purpose does this serve?

Making the correct choice: I or me?

When using the pronouns *I* or *me*, try reading the sentence with just the pronoun and the verb. Use the pronoun that fits when it is by itself.

> Mary and *I work* part-time at the theatre.
>
> **not**
>
> Mary and me work part-time at the theatre.

Be careful of he/she or they.

When using pronouns such as *he*, *she*, or *they* (or *his/hers/their*), make sure the plural form (*they*) is used only when referring to more than one person.

> When *someone* has been drinking, *he/she* is more likely to get in an accident.
>
> **not**
>
> When *someone* has been drinking, *they* are more likely to get in an accident.

Plural needs plural.

The pronoun and the verb need to match.

> *Several* people *are* already here.

Singular needs singular.

Singular pronouns, such as *someone, anyone,* and *nobody,* are needed when the verb is singular.

> *Nobody is* allowed to leave the building.

Avoid double negatives.

If more than one word like *no, never, not, can't, hardly,* or *neither* is used, the meaning becomes reversed.

> She is so tired she *can hardly* keep her eyes open.
>
> **not**
>
> She is so tired she *can't hardly* keep her eyes open.

Keep the tense the same.

If the writing uses the past tense (e.g., was, did, forgot, ran, bought, told) keep it consistent as long as the same time frame is being discussed.

> Yesterday the teacher told me...
>
> **not**
>
> Yesterday the teacher tells me...

Citing References

When students conduct research or use other sources—books, articles, web text, etc.—as part of the writing process, they need to know how to include direct quotes in their own writing in a way that recognizes the original author. In-text citations tell the reader that this portion of the writing came from another source. Here are some suggestions for effectively including quotes:

- Name the author in a lead up to the quote, then provide the page reference.

> John Doe reported that volcanoes in the Pacific were, "currently active and could erupt any day" (53).

- Include the author's name and page number following the quote.

> "Volcanoes in the Pacific are currently active and could erupt any day" (Doe 53).

- If there are four or more authors, record the following after the quote: the first author's name followed by et al. and the page reference.

> "Volcanoes in the Pacific are currently active and could erupt any day" (Doe et al. 53).

- If the author is unknown, include the full title in a phrase leading up to the quote, or use a shortened title and page number after the quote

> In *Mountains of Destruction* it is reported that volcanoes in the Pacific are "currently active and could erupt any day" (53).
>
> **or**
>
> "Volcanoes in the Pacific are currently active and could erupt any day" (*Mountains of Destruction* 53).

- If you are using an electronic source, use the same rules as for a print source. You might not be able to include an author or page number, as many web sites do not include this kind of information.

Bibliography

All research reports should include a bibliography or a list of works that have been cited.

- Place the bibliography at the end of the piece of writing on its own page.
- Include any works that have been directly cited, or that have been used for general reference.
- Arrange entries alphabetically by the authors' last names.
- Don't indent the first line, but indent any other lines of the citation.
- If your work is typed, use italics to indicate the title of a book source; if the piece is handwritten, underline the title.
- Use quotation marks to indicate the title of an article.

Follow standard protocol for bibliography entries.

- A book (one author): record last name followed by first name.

> Doe, John. *Mountains of Destruction.* Someplace: Publisher Name, 2004.

- Two or three authors: list authors in alphabetical order. For second and third authors, record first then last name.

> Doe, John, Jane Smith, and Joe Thompson. *Mountains of Destruction.* Someplace: Publisher Name, 2004.

- Four or more authors: list the first author followed by *et al.*

> Doe, John, et al. *Mountains of Destruction.* Someplace: Publisher Name, 2004.

- Unknown author: begin with the title (omit the first word if it is *The*, *An*, or *A*)

> *Mountains of Destruction.* Someplace: Publisher Name, 2004.

- Articles in a magazine: include volume number and page numbers.

> Doe, John. "Mountains of Destruction." *GeoMag* Oct. 2004: 12-14.

- Article in a newspaper: include date and page number

> Doe, John. "Mountains of Destruction." *The Post* 18 Oct. 2004: A4.

- Web site: include title of site, date, and URL.

> "Mountains of Destruction." *GeoSite.* 18 October 2004. Internet. http://www.website.com.

Creating a Title Page

A title page is a simple but varied component of student writing. Many teachers have different expectations when it comes to how a title page should be organized. In some cases a title page is not required, nor should it be. If a student has completed a piece of written work that is being shared with others, it may require a title page; if it is simply a quick draft or a piece of daily homework, such a formality may not be necessary.

Most students know that a title page must include the following:

- title
- student's name
- date
- course or subject

In some cases the teacher's name and an illustration or other creative element are required.

The tricky part for the student comes in remembering where on the title page each of these pieces of information should be placed. The samples below are but two examples, and are by no means the only ways of arranging a title page.

Title

Author's Name

Date

Teacher's Name

Course

Title

Author's Name

Date

Course

Across the Curriculum

In an effort to support students, make a team decision about how title pages should look, and then post a sample in the classroom, or provide a sample for students to keep in their binders, that they can refer to as necessary. Making the requirements consistent across subject areas—and, if possible, grade levels—can be helpful to your students.

Pictures, Charts, Graphs, and Other Visuals: Supporting and Extending the Learning

Word Wise

visual
photo
illustration
diagram
cut-away
chart
timeline
table
graph
scatter plot
map

In the content areas, visual supports—pictures, charts, graphs, etc.—are more than just extras. These visuals are often central to the text and its ability to convey meaning. The processes involved in constructing visual text are much the same as those involved in creating a piece of print text.

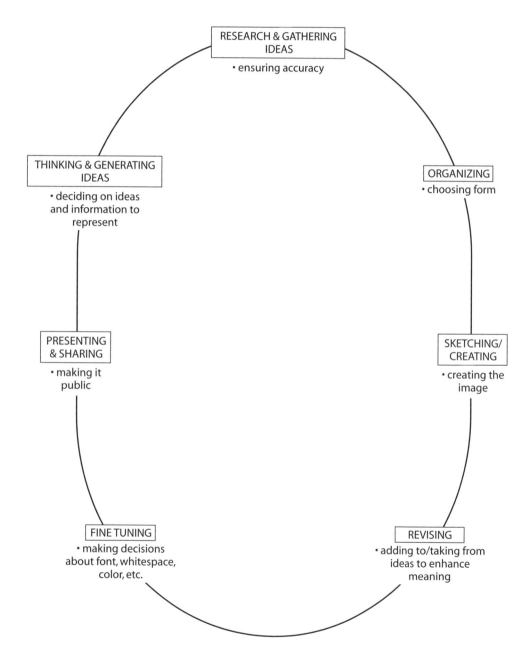

RESEARCH & GATHERING IDEAS
• ensuring accuracy

ORGANIZING
• choosing form

SKETCHING/ CREATING
• creating the image

REVISING
• adding to/taking from ideas to enhance meaning

FINE TUNING
• making decisions about font, whitespace, color, etc.

PRESENTING & SHARING
• making it public

THINKING & GENERATING IDEAS
• deciding on ideas and information to represent

The following pages outline a variety of types of visuals that students may create in support of writing across the curriculum. The general purpose of the visual is identified followed by its basic components, and an example is provided. Rather than simply providing students with completed samples, offer them the Visual Options chart on page 91 in Appendix, along with samples of visuals specific to the curriculum. Ask them to examine the samples and complete the chart by identifying the purpose and components of each sample. The examples can be generated by the students, and the charts can be posted in the classroom or kept in the students' notebook for future reference.

Visual: Photo

Purpose
- used to capture real objects
- shows something exactly as it appears
- recorded with a camera

Components
- subject, background, foreground
- may include a heading, caption, color

Visual: Illustration

Purpose
- a person's impression of an image complete with background
- often depicts a location and the objects, people, and other living things present
- created by hand or with a computer

Components
- subject, background, foreground
- may include a heading, caption, color

Visual: Diagram

Purpose
- explains or shows how something works or is constructed
- is often used to show what is not evident through photos or illustrations
- includes only the main subject and essential details

Components
- heading, subject/object, labels, arrows, caption, legend
- may include color

Visual: Cross Section or Cut-away

Purpose
- shows the inside of an object that is not ordinarily visible
- explains the composition or inner workings of something

Components

- heading, subject (outside with portion of inside visible), labels, arrows, a caption
- may include overlays and color

Visual: Chart

Purpose

- shows relationships and presents information in an organized fashion
- can be a flow chart, graphic organizer, etc.

Components

- heading, text, lines, columns and rows, a caption
- may include arrows and color or shading

Visual: Timeline

Purpose

- the chronology or a sequence of events

Components

- heading, arrow of time divided into equal increments, labels, caption
- may include pictures aligned with labels and text

Visual: Table

Purpose

- presents information in an accessible format that aids comparison

Components

- headings (may also include units of measurement), columns, rows, data/information, a caption
- may include bullets, color or shading

Visual: Bar Graph

Purpose

- shows relationships between the subject and quantity
- shows the quantity of various items/categories
- contains discrete data
- aids comparison

Components

- heading, x-axis, y-axis, labels, units of measure, equal increments, numbers, color or shading, legend
- may include a caption

Visual: Line Graph

Purpose

- shows relationships between the subject and quantity
- shows how the quantity of one item changes over time
- contains continuous data
- multiple lines on the same graph can be used to show multiple items for comparison

Components

- heading, x-axis, y-axis, labels, units of measure, equal increments, numbers, legend, caption
- may include color

Visual: Pie Graph

Purpose

- shows the proportion or quantity of the subject relative to the sum total

Components

- heading, labels, color or shading, legend
- may include a caption

Visual: Scatter Plot

Purpose

- shows the quantity of various items
- amounts are discrete and do not show continuous data

Components

- heading, x-axis, y-axis, labels, units of measure, equal increments, numbers, legend
- may include a caption and color

Visual: Map

Purpose

- shows location and other patterns (e.g., places, climate, population, resources)

Components

- heading, scale, compass, color or shading, symbols, legend, caption
- may include a grid

PART 2

Purposes of Writing

Writing should always be done with a purpose in mind. The most basic purpose associated with writing is to communicate ideas or information to others. This basic purpose can then be refined to include intentions such as to persuade or convince, to describe, to explain, to compare, to respond, and so on. Once the writer has established a clear purpose for writing, he/she has a framework for the writing. This framework will help establish form and organization.

In this part you will find key words, practical strategies, and ideas organized around innovative ways to incorporate different types of writing into your classroom instruction.

Patterns of Writing: Matching Structure to Purpose
Painting Pictures with Words: Writing that Describes
Presenting the Facts: The Informational Report
Persuasive Writing: The Importance of Supporting Opinions
Procedural Writing: Documenting a Sequence
Pros and Cons: Comparative Writing
Personal Writing: Sharing Thoughts, Ideas, and Reactions
Poetry: A Way of Knowing
Posters: Creating Visual Texts
Pamphlets, Folders, and 3D Models: Other Ways to Present Information

Patterns of Writing: Matching Structure to Purpose

Word Wise

purpose
descriptive
informational
persuasive
procedural
sequential
comparative
personal

See also charts on pages 92–93 in Appendix E.

Over the next few pages, different kinds of writing are presented in chart form, with examples. Consider using these or other samples as models with your students, and complete a similar chart after examining the writing samples.

Descriptive writing	Example
Framework • Begins with a general statement that identifies the topic • Ideas are described in such a way that the reader can envision the topic. • Language appeals to the five senses and helps to paint the picture. **Examples** observations examples connections comments questions predictions **key words** sensory words	**My Rock** The rock was small; about the size of a toy car. You could hold it easily in your hand. It felt rough and chalky, like there was a fine residue on its surface. The edges of the rock were jagged and sharp. It had obviously chipped off a larger rock and had not weathered much yet. The color of the rock was white. When you looked closely you could see small flecks or crystals that looked shiny or clear. There were some brown streaks in the rock too.

Informational writing	Example
Framework • Begins with a general statement that identifies the topic • Each paragraph describes one of the subtopics. • Ideas are presented factually. • Language is neutral and impersonal. **Examples** reports essays **key words** technical terms	**Ramadan** Ramadan is an Islamic holy month that is recognized by Muslims world wide. Ramadan is always the ninth month of the Islamic lunar calendar, so it falls on different dates each year. During Ramadan Muslims fast during daylight. They do not eat, drink or smoke tobacco from sunrise to sunset. Each day begins before dawn with a meal called *Sahoor* and ends after dusk with a meal called *Iftar*. Prayers are also an important part of the Muslim faith and part of Ramadan. Each day begins with prayers from the *Qu'ran* (Koran). Throughout the day there are 5 daily prayers. When Ramadan is over, there will be a feast known as *Id al-Fitr*. Family and friends will get together to share presents and eat fancy foods. Ramadan is a time for Muslims to feel closer to their families, to the poor, to their communities, and to their faith.

Persuasive writing	Example

Framework

- Begins by stating the topic and position
- Ideas or opinions are then supported with evidence or a convincing argument.
- Often includes statistics, reasoning, and use of emotional or strong language
- May include possible counter arguments and the rationale for their ineffectiveness
- Concludes by reiterating the initial argument and position

Examples

letters to the editor
proposals
judgments or arguments
advertisements
résumés

key words

must
essential
superlatives (*most, greatest, least*)
testimonials (*research shows, experts say*)

The European Union: A Great Idea

The rest of the world can learn a lot from the European Union. The European Union was formed after a lengthy evolution, and presently includes 15 countries. This Union and the resulting cooperation have had many benefits for the citizens of its member countries, as well as benefits for non-citizens. It has been so successful that other continents such as Africa, Asia, and South America would be wise to consider such a Union.

One of the greatest benefits of the EU has been economic. It has resulted in the elimination of all tariffs between member countries, and as a result the volume of trade among member countries has increased substantially. It has been so successful that the combined imports and exports of the EU are greater than any single country in the world. Because of increased trade, citizens have also enjoyed an increased standard of living. In continents such as Africa, South America, and Asia, where the standard of living is much lower, such a move towards cooperation would certainly improve the lives of the people.

Freedom of movement has also improved for EU citizens. Anyone who is a citizen of an EU country can live and work anywhere in the Union. This freedom also allows them to vote in any Union or local election in the country in which they live (even if they are not a citizen of that country). This has definitely resulted in the people having a greater say in the governing of their own and nearby nations.

Freedom has also been a benefit for tourists. Open borders and a common currency have made travel from country to country much easier. Tourists no longer have to go through customs or convert money as they leave one country and go to another. This freedom and ease of travel means more people are likely to travel to Europe, further boosting the economy and the quality of life.

Procedural/Sequential writing	Example

Framework

- Begins with a goal or purpose
- Is sequential or linear in nature, explaining the steps or process involved
- Each step or part of the process is easily identified and clearly explains the event or task.

How to Play Video Games

Everyone loves video games. Playing video games is easy. To get started you have to set up the machine. First off, you plug the console into the TV. After you do that, plug the controller into the console. Next, turn on the TV and the console. Now you are ready to put the game into the console. After waiting for it to load, you press Start on your controller. Now you are ready to have fun.

or

Examples

timelines
directions/instructions
lab reports

key words

first
next
following
finally

Magic Raisins

1. Add 5ml of baking soda to 250 ml of water.
2. Stir until the baking soda is dissolved.
3. Add 6-7 raisins.
4. Add 25 ml of vinegar
5. Observe
6. Record observations

Comparative writing	Example

Framework

- Begins by identifying the items to be compared and possible criteria for comparison
- Describes the qualities or characteristics of the individual items, and explains their similarities and differences

Examples

consumer reports
metaphors
analogies

key words

unlike
just as
more
most
words ending in *-er*

Comparing Fast Food Options

When asked to consider the best options for fast food there are many things one must consider. Top of this list of considerations are taste, variety, and value.

The first and most important consideration to true food lovers is the taste or quality of the food being served. Burger joints generally offer a half dozen standard burgers, many of which are pre-made and waiting for you when you step up to the counter. Pizza shops prepare the pizza once you have placed the order and allow the customer to choose the toppings. Likewise, your sub is made to order. However, in the case of a sub, it is usually made right in front of you.

A second factor to consider is variety or options. In the case of burgers, your variety is often limited to the size or number of patties and a few basic toppings. Pizza, while it offers choice of toppings, is essentially the same product: a round piece of dough with sauce and a combination of meat and vegetables chopped and spread over the top. Sub shops provide even greater opportunity for individuality. Here the choices begin with the type of bread, and also include the main filling, toppings, and any sauces your heart desires. This choice gives the customer the chance to ask for more of this and less of that in an effort to create the perfect sandwich.

Finally one must consider price. In this category, burger joints are generally the best option. In most cases you can get a simple burger for around a dollar. Even the smallest pizza will cost you at least 5 to 10 dollars; that is, unless you can buy your pizza by the slice, where you are compromising taste and variety in the name of price. Subs, while not as cheap as burgers, do offer the chance to earn "frequent buyer points" and ultimately get you something everyone wants—a free sub.

In conclusion, it seems obvious that when one considers taste, variety, and price, the best bet is a sub. Tasty, made to order just the way you like it, and with a chance to get free food, subs are the way to go. Try one. I think you'll like it.

Personal writing	Example

Framework
 	
• Begins with the date and topic
• Proceeds to describe the topic, event, or idea from a personal point of view
• May include likes and dislikes, opinions, suggestions
• Opinions should be supported with a rational and evidence
• May include visual forms of representation such as sketches, charts, etc.
 	
Examples
 	
diaries
journals
self-assessments
logs
reflections on learning
opinion pieces
 	
key words
 	
I think…
I believe…
I learned…
I wonder…
This reminds me of…
	May 27, 2005
	
	   Today in science we learned about fluids. We had to put 4 different fluids on 3 different surfaces (tin foil, plastic wrap, waxed paper) and observe them. I noticed that each of the fluids behaved a little differently on each of the pieces of paper. The fluids kept their shape the best on the tin foil. On the waxed paper they kind of soaked in.
	
	   One of the things I wondered is if it would have made a difference if we had used the other side of the tin foil (we used the shiny side)?
	
	   We also poured the left-overs all together in a glass. They looked like this:
	
	I think the fluids we used were:
	   A- maple syrup
	   B- liquid dish soap
	   C- cooking oil
	   D- red wine vinegar 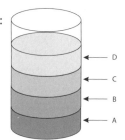

Painting Pictures with Words: Writing that Describes

Consider the social studies classroom where you want students to describe a period in history, an event, or a significant person; or a science classroom where students are to describe an observation or a scientific phenomenon. Whether this description is to be put on paper or shared orally with the class, you hope that what the student shares will be descriptive and detailed enough to create an accurate image or picture in the minds of his/her audience. Helping students develop the skills necessary to write or create this kind of picture can be done quickly; it can reinforce the conceptual understanding you want to foster in the student, as well as supporting the student's skill as a writer.

Descriptive writing is rich in descriptive language. It is writing that creates a picture and appeals to the senses. As historians, anthropologists, geographers, biologists, chemists, geologists, etc., the ability to describe something with detail, accuracy, and richness is essential to passing along information that furthers the study of that topic.

Across the Curriculum

Possible topics for writing descriptive text for content areas include

Social Studies
- a period of history (life during the Depression)
- a place (Africville, Nova Scotia; the Sahara desert)

Science
- a nearby ecosystem (pond, tidal pool)
- the appearance of a plant cell or animal cell

Health
- an example of bullying
- an example of racism

Math
- various geometric shapes
- information shown on a graph

The first step in producing writing that is descriptive is keen observation. Observation is a key scientific process and one that students are expected to develop as part of the science program and curriculum. Communicating what is observed requires the careful selection of words that will help to create a picture in the reader's mind. To help students create these written pictures, consider scaffolding the process.

Give students the opportunity to observe something firsthand and ask them to record words that describe what they see. If the school is close to the ocean, perhaps students could be asked to make as many observations as possible about a tidal pool. Another idea might be to observe a plant, a rock, an earthworm, or a suspension bridge. Initially it is wise to begin with a relatively small area/object for observation, so students can really focus on the details. Initial descriptions will probably focus on more obvious characteristics:

- size
- color
- number/quantity
- shape
- location/position

Once the student has recorded words to describe these initial observations provide them with some more complex criteria for observation, such as

- texture
- smells
- sounds
- background/surroundings
- point of view/perspective
- movement
- mood

This second round of observation is intended to plunge the student deeper into his/her study. Follow up provides the opportunity to discuss the kind of language used, the importance of appropriate measurements to describe size and quantity, and the learning that has occurred. As well, the documentation, or list of descriptions, serves as a word bank, a foundation for future writing.

Focusing on Observations

Another great way to have students look at word choice and the way they write observations is to have them complete a short experiment and record their observations. Here is a simple science experiment:

Magic Raisins.

1. Add 5 ml of baking soda to 250 ml of water.
2. Stir until the baking soda is dissolved.
3. Add 6–7 raisins.
4. Add 25 ml of vinegar
5. Observe
6. Record observations.

Once students have a number of observations written, ask them to look over their observations and choose one that is strong, or precise and detailed. Ask the student to consider why it is strong. Does it convey accurately and with detail a picture of what has been observed? Next, ask the students to choose one observation that they feel needs work. Perhaps it is too vague. This observation is one that needs to be revised.

If the observation is

> *The raisins were moving around.*

Try changing the verb so it is more specific:

> *The raising were floating and sinking.*

Then, add two or three details:

> *The raisins floated to the top of the solution. Gas bubbles surrounding the raisin burst. Then the raisin sank back to the bottom.*

Next, change the order of the parts:

> *The many gas bubbles surrounding the raisins caused the raisins to float to the top of the solution. Some of the bubbles burst at the surface, and then the raisin sank back to the bottom.*

Observing the World in Pictures

In the social studies classroom, firsthand observation may not always be possible; the use of photographs can help accomplish the same thing. *National Geographic* magazine is a source of many great photographs, as are old calendars and books. Students can even use their textbooks for this activity.

1. Select a photograph or piece of artwork that shows something that relates to the unit of study. The best pictures are those that show at least one person. Make sure that every student has access to the photograph: make photocopies, use a transparency, or choose something that is in the textbook.
2. Ask students to look at the photo and make a list of 10 nouns they see in the picture. These nouns may be either objects they see (e.g., gun, mud, soldier, helmet) or nouns that represent ideas or concepts that are not tangible (e.g., war, fear, homesickness, gunfire). Each students writes 10 short sentences using the nouns.
3. Each student then combines the ten sentences to make five longer sentences.
4. Each student writes a short dialogue between characters in the photo, or a monologue of a character's inner thoughts.
5. Finally, the student combines his/her five sentences and the dialogue, reviews what he/she has written, and rearranges and makes any adjustments to the writing to make a seamless piece of text that describes that photo and that moment in history.

Steps 1 and 2:

1. trench—The trench was wet.
2. soldiers—The soldiers took cover.
3. helmet—Green metal helmets covered their heads.
4. letter—He wrote a letter to his sweetheart.
5. gun—His gun was loaded and ready.
6. homesickness—He suffered from homesickness.
7. disease—You could smell death and disease in the air.
8. doom—A feeling of doom closed in.
9. pride—His family felt pride and worry.
10. explosions—Constant explosions filled the air.

Step 3:

1. The trench was wet and dirty; you could smell death and disease in the air.
2. Leaning against a mud wall, the soldier took cover and wrote a letter to his sweetheart.
3. He felt nothing but homesickness, and his family felt a mixture of pride and worry.
4. With a green metal helmet and loaded gun, he was ready to fight.
5. Constant explosions filled the air, and a feeling of doom closed in.

Step 4:

"Hey, Jack! You writing home again?"

"Sure am! It's the only thing that keeps me going. How about you? You got anyone special back home?"

"Me? Nah, not really."

Step 5:

"Hey, Jack! You writing home again?"

"Sure am! It's the only thing that keeps me going. How about you? You got anyone special back home?"

"Me? Nah, not really."

The trench was wet and dirty; you could smell death and disease in the air. Leaning against a mud wall, the soldier wrote a letter to his sweetheart. It was one of many he had written. He felt nothing but homesickness, and his family felt a mixture of pride and worry.

With a green metal helmet and loaded gun, he was ready to fight. Or was he? Constant explosions filled the air, and a feeling of doom closed in. All he wanted was to be home, home with his family and his girl—home where it was warm and dry, where he could think and feel something other than the numbness of war.

Presenting the Facts: The Informational Report

Word Wise

report
details
matrix

The informational report is perhaps the most commonly assigned writing task for students in the middle or junior-high years. This kind of writing involves the ability to communicate, in a factual manner, essential or important information about a topic. It also requires the student to be able to organize this information appropriately. For many students the challenge of ensuring that information is accurate and organized in its presentation poses a challenge.

Across the Curriculum

Possible topics for writing informational text for content areas include

Social Studies
  • an event (the Montgomery bus boycott, the trial of Louis Reil)
  • an issue (world poverty, globalization)
  • the life of a famous person (Malcom X, Nelly McLung)

Science
  • various structures (kinds of bridges)
  • types of volcanoes

Health
  • the human heart and how it works
  • eating disorders and their effects

Math
  • contributions of a famous mathematician
  • mathematical concept (fractions)

List–Group–Label

See List–Group–Label (page 94).

The list–group–label process is one that works well when assisting students with the organization of ideas prior to writing an informational report. The template in Appendix F can be used by students to complete this part of the task. In a math class, for example, students may be asked to write a report about fractions. The List box is where students can record all their ideas. These may be individual words or phrases related to the topic, and they can be recorded in the order that they come to mind. Next, these words are grouped and placed in the Group columns. In the case of fractions, students may choose to place all the ideas specific to the different kinds of fractions in the first column, operations using fractions in the second column, the relationship to decimals in the third, and real-world examples of using fractions in the fourth. Finally, labels are given to each group and recorded above the appropriate column.

numerator	share something	invert and multiply
denominator	cooking	add
simple fraction	measurement	subtract
reduce	mixed	whole
part	mixed	multiply
least common multiple	improper	divide
Kinds/Parts	**Operations**	**Everyday Use**
simple	invert and multiply	cooking
mixed	least common multiple	measurement
improper	reduce	sharing
part	add	
whole	subtract	
numerator	multiply	
denominator	divide	

Understanding fractions is an important skill. You need to know the kinds of fractions, how to use them, and their application in everyday life.

There are three basic kinds of fractions. A simple fraction is the most common. Fractions like 1/2 or 5/8 are simple fractions. They have a numerator, or top number, and a denominator, or bottom number. The denominator represents the total number of parts of an object. The numerator is the number of parts being counted. For example, someone may eat 3/4 of an apple. This means the apple was divided into four equal parts and the person ate three of them. The second kind of fraction is a mixed fraction. This is a whole number and a fraction, for example 1 1/2, or 3 1/4. The third kind is an improper fraction. This is a fraction where the numerator is larger than the denominator such as, 5/4 or 10/8.

When you are working with fractions you need to know how to add, subtract, multiply and divide them. In order to do these operations you need to know some other things. Before you can add or subtract fractions you need to make sure they have the same denominator. 1/5 and 2/5 can be added by adding the numerators and keeping the denominator the same. 1/2 and 2/6 can not be added as they are. First you need to find the lowest common multiple of the denominators. In this case it is 6. 1/2 is the same as 3/6 so this can then be added to 2/6. After solving a problem with fractions you need to reduce it to its simplest form. The fraction 8/10 can be reduced to 4/5 because both 8 and 10 can be divided by 2.

Fractions are important in everyday life because we use them in measurement and in cooking. Many of the ingredients in a recipe are written as fractions. It is also good to understand fractions so you can share things with others. Dividing a pizza or a chocolate bar among friends means using fractions.

Writing the Informational Report/Essay

The framework students create using the List–Group–Label template will support the organization and development of an piece of informational writing. The following hints will help students turn the template into a well-organized report/essay.

- Each Group (column) of ideas forms a paragraph in the body of the report/essay.
- Each Label can be used to create a lead sentence for the corresponding paragraph.
- All of the Labels combined can be used to create an introductory paragraph.
- The concluding paragraph should reiterate the main topic and may reference the Labels.

Using the Report Matrix

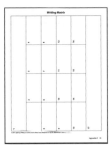

See Writing Matrix (page 95).

One of the skills we expect students to demonstrate is the ability to write an informational report. In some cases, this expectation is met with frustration and disappointment. For students who are unsure how to go about organizing and writing such a report, the steps listed below can be helpful.

1. Identify a topic or research question. Write it in cell 1.
2. Select two or more subtopics. Record these along the top row in cells 2, 3, 4.
3. Decide on aspects for research. Record in the first column in cells 5, 9, 13.
4. Record factual information in each of cells 6, 7, 8; 10, 11, 12; 14, 15, 16.
5. Record a summary statement in cell 17.
6. Use the outline to transform the information into a series of cohesive paragraphs. Each vertical column becomes a paragraph.

Paragraph 1: Introduction
- lead sentence: cell 1
- paragraph sentences: cells 2, 3, 4

Paragraph 2: First Idea
- lead sentence: cell 2
- paragraph sentences: cells 6, 10, 14

Paragraph 3: Second Idea
- lead sentence: cell 3
- paragraph sentences: cells 7, 11, 15

Paragraph 4: Third Idea
- lead sentence: cell 4
- paragraph sentences: cells 8, 12, 16

Paragraph 5: Conclusion
- cell 17

1 The role of women during wartime			
Subtopics → Research ↓	2 WWI	3 WWII	4 present day
5 On the battle front	6 • Automatically rejected for overseas duty • 3,000+ joined Canadian army nursing services and worked behind the lines	7 • 50,000 women enlisted for duty, at home and overseas • Roles include nursing, flying planes, driving vehicles, running communications equipment, admin/support work	8 • All roles open to women
9 In the home	10 • Knitted socks, gloves, scarves • Made bandages • Sent packages to troops	11 • Rationing & shortages of food and supplies • Saved metal, paper, rubber, glass	12 • No role for civilian women
13 In the workforce	14 • Took over men's jobs: factory work (e.g., munitions), civil service, banks & offices • Paid less & expected to leave when men returned	15 • Took over jobs from men (twice as many women in the workforce at the end of the war) • Fighting for standard rates of pay	16 • Equal pay for equal work • All sectors open to women • Not directly affected by war
17 Significant change in the role of women during wartime			

Across the Curriculum

A similar matrix can be used to organize a comparative essay (see page 52). Rather than each paragraph being constructed from the vertical columns of the matrix, each horizontal row is written into its own paragraph.

Persuasive Writing: The Importance of Supporting Opinions

Word Wise

persuasive
point of view
opinion
evidence
bias

Young people are rarely without an opinion. The challenge is to teach them how to support these opinions. The goal of persuasive writing is for the writer to convince others to agree with his/her position on a particular topic. The more support a writer can give for his/her position or argument, the more likely others will be persuaded. The activities outlined below are intended to help students develop the skills necessary to write effective persuasive text.

When teaching students how to identify a topic or point of view, or how to examine a piece of text for word choice, it his helpful to introduce it first as a shared experience. This means you will facilitate the learning experience and seek input from the students as you try to help them understand the concept. Making an overhead of the text and sharing it with all students provides a common experience and is a good way to generate discussion and elicit input.

Across the Curriculum

Possible topics for writing persuasive text for content areas include

Social Studies
- personal responsibility and human rights
- Is globalization good?
- writing a speech in role (politician, activist, military general)

Science
- genetically modified foods
- burning of fossil fuels/sources of energy
- importance of space exploration

Health
- taxation of sporting goods
- smoking laws
- same-sex marriage laws

Math
- importance of math in everyday situations
- nominations for the figure who made the greatest contribution to math
- defending the solution to a word problem

One of the best ways to help students write persuasive text (or any text) is to provide them with models. Persuasive text is easily available in newspapers and magazines. Have students read letters to the editor from the local newspaper. The best time to do this is following a high-profile or controversial event. The days following Halloween can provide letters by individuals expressing their opinions about the occasion.

1. First, have students read through a variety of letters and try to identify the topic and point of view of the author.
2. Then the students can read carefully to see how authors organize their letter. Most letters state an opinion and then give reasons to support that opinion. In many cases this support is based on personal experience or facts the writer has collected from another source. Authors of persuasive text may also give suggestions related to how to improve or change a given situation.
3. The final step is to do an even closer read, focusing on word choice. Ask students to circle or highlight any words or phrases that are emotional or convincing. Using this information, students can make a graphic organizer to assist in writing persuasive letters, along with a series of powerful word posters.

Say It Like You Mean It

Persuasive writing requires that writers think carefully about the words they use. Word choice can make a statement sound stronger and more forceful, or softer and less forceful.

Share the following sentences with students and ask if all four sentences communicate the same information. What are the similarities and what are the differences? Students should be able to identify that all four sentences deal with the same topic: protection of the environment. All four sentences take a similar stance; that is, they say that protection of the environment is necessary. What is different is the strength or the forcefulness of the position.

- I think you should take action to protect our environment.
- You must take action to protect our environment
- I think you should take action now to protect our environment.
- It is essential that you take immediate action to protect our environment.

Ask students to look carefully at the words chosen by the author. Many of the words are the same; however, each sentence has some words that make the position softer or stronger. Have a discussion about these words and the impact they have on the reader. Which sentences are stronger or more forceful? Why?

Next, have students choose a piece of persuasive text and look carefully at the words used. Have them discuss in pairs the implied meaning of each. They might list words according to how important the message they convey seems:

Word that Show Lesser Importance: *can, may, should, I think*, etc.

Words that Show Greater Importance: *really, extremely, must, essential, research proves, scientists say*, etc.

Words that Show Time: *urgent, now, immediate*, etc.

Finally, challenge the students to "say it like you mean it." Together the students must revise the passage to include more forceful, or less forceful, language.

Above and Below Bias

Above and Below bias is a similar activity in which students look carefully at word choice and the impact it has on the meaning of the piece of text.

1. Select a passage and identify a number of words that, if changed, could affect the overall message. Underline these words and provide a copy of the passage to each student.
2. Divide the students into two groups: Above and Below. Explain that both groups must select alternatives for each of the words that are underlined. The Above group will choose words that give the piece a more positive spin and write each new word above the original one. The Below group is to choose words that have a more negative connotation and record each of these below the original word. It may be helpful to have students work in groups to complete the task, and then mix or change the groups so they can share and discuss the impact of word choice.

Argument–Evidence–Source

See Argument–Evidence–Source (page 96).

The template for Argument–Evidence–Source assists students with locating and using evidence to support arguments in their persuasive writing. The template simply serves as an outline to help the student remember that each argument must be supported with evidence, and that the source of the evidence must be recorded. This template can be used by a reader to make notes about a piece of persuasive text that is being read, or it can be used by a writer to make notes about a piece that he/she will eventually write. The instructions below are intended to help students examine a piece of persuasive text.

1. Following the first read through, ask students to identify the Argument or opinion being expressed. Each argument that is presented in the article can be recorded in a cell in the first column of the chart. It is important that each be written as a singular argument, as this will make the selection of evidence much easier.
2. Next students are asked to try and locate within the article Evidence to support each argument or point of view.
3. Once students have completed the first two columns, they can then record the Source.

Evidence and support for one's argument can come in many different forms:
- facts and figures (statistics)
- testimonials (quotes from famous people or qualified experts)
- personal experience (your own stories)
- quotes (lines taken directly from a text)
- examples (real world occurrences)

Creating an Outline From a Shared Text

See Hitting the Target template (page 97).

This Argument–Evidence–Source graphic organizer can be used by students to help them construct their own persuasive essay. Before the students complete the essay, take them back to the earlier learning activity to set criteria. What did they notice about other persuasive essays?

Use the information from the Argument–Evidence–Source graphic organizer and a target of criteria to help students visualize what it is they are trying to achieve. A target is most effective if generated with students, but with final input by the teacher. For example, here are four basic criteria:

- Argument is clear.
- At least two pieces of evidence are given for each Argument.
- Evidence supports the Argument.
- A minimum of two sources are used for evidence.

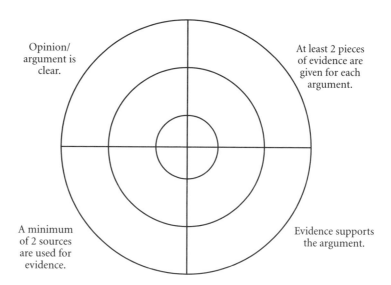

Additional criteria may include

- Mechanics are strong: this includes spelling, punctuation, and sentence structure.
- Organization and paragraphing is evident: introductory paragraph states the position; each argument and supporting evidence forms a paragraph; a concluding paragraph reiterates position.

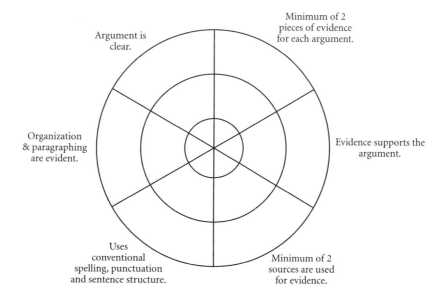

For more information on criteria, see "Providing Specific Feedback" on page 68.

Procedural Writing: Documenting a Sequence

Word Wise

procedural
sequential
science lab

Procedural text is frequently encountered in the sciences. Each time a student must complete a lab report, or explain what they did or how they did it, they are using procedural writing.

Across the Curriculum

Possible topics for writing procedural text for content areas include

Social Studies
- how to make a map
- locating information in a book or atlas
- how to conduct an interview

Science
- steps in a science experiment
- using science equipment such as a beam balance or microscope
- preparing wet mount slides

Health
- safety steps prior to an activity
- decision-making steps
- how to do rescue breathing or CPR

Math
- how to solve an algebraic equation
- solving word problems
- constructing a graph

One of the challenges we face is helping students write not just procedural text, but text that is interesting and engaging. Younger students, or those with limited experiences in writing, may churn out procedural text that is nothing but statements strung together with *I... Then I... Then... Then I....* Here are some activities to help students create procedural texts.

Examine examples

Find examples of procedural texts that show variety: a numbered list of steps; a paragraph that uses sequential language (e.g., first, next, finally); a series of steps in paragraph form that are written without numbers or in sequential language, but for which the order and spacing indicate sequence. Give the examples to students and ask them to look at how they have been written.

Vary your vocabulary

The word "then" may be the most overused word in procedural text. Ask students to brainstorm a list of alternatives to the word "then." Create a poster and post it on the classroom wall for future reference. Make the poster a "living" poster: encourage students to add to it throughout the year as they think of alternatives to the word "then."

Use a numbered list to organize ideas

The following activity offers students a higher level of support and is good for introducing the concept of procedural text.

1. Choose a topic that pertains to something you are studying in class, or encourage students to choose a topic of their own.
2. Provide students with cue cards or squares of paper that are numbered.
3. Have students record one step on each card.
4. Cards should then be spaced out in sequence.
5. Students can share their sequences and through discussion determine if any changes need to be made to the order, or if additional steps are required.
6. Once the students are satisfied with the sequence and the level of detail, the steps can be rewritten if necessary.

Putting It All Together

See Putting It All Together (page 98).

This activity can be done to follow up on what students have learned in the previous activities, or can be done in place of them. Using the graphic organizer provided, students will go through three steps to write a paragraph that is organized in a sequential form.

1. Ask students to brainstorm key words that can be used to signal sequence or procedure. These words should be written at top left as "Alternatives to using *then.*"
2. Ask the student to select a "How to" topic, or provide a topic for him/her. From this topic, students will establish steps showing "How to..." Steps should be recorded in sequence using the numbered list.
3. The student uses the steps and the sequence words to write a paragraph in the right half of the chart explaining "How to..." Encourage the student to use as many of the sequence words as possible. Remind the student that the paragraph needs to begin with a strong lead that captures the readers' attention, tells what the paragraph is about, and makes them want to read on. A concluding sentence at the end is a good idea.

Writing a Science Lab

See Components of a Lab Report (page 99).

Every time a student reads the directions for an experiment or creates a lab report, she/he is encountering procedural text. One of our challenges is helping students develop the language necessary to understand and construct this kind of writing. The chart on page 99 shows the four main sections of a science lab report. The Purpose or Explanation section outlines how students write procedural text in order to explain what they did. Vocabulary that may be used in each of the sections is suggested. Helping students understand and use this vocabulary is essential.

Pros and Cons: Comparative Writing

Word Wise

comparison
pros
cons
similarity
metaphor
analogy

Comparative writing is writing that describes the similarities and differences of two or more ideas or things. Comparative writing can be challenging because many students have the tendency to simply describe the items individually, without offering a comparison. By comparing, a student demonstrates a higher level of thinking that requires comprehension, analysis, and evaluation, and the expression of these ideas through writing. The activities are intended to support students as they learn how to create comparative texts.

Across the Curriculum

Possible topics for writing comparative text for content areas include

Social Studies
• kinds of government
• land forms
• cultures

Science
• biotic vs abiotic
• types of rocks (sedimentary, igneous, metamorphic)
• properties of various fluids

Health
• diseases
• kinds of drugs
• advertising techniques

Math
• mixed, improper, and proper fractions
• geometric shapes
• kinds of graphs

Pro and Con

The ability to look at a topic critically or to see a single topic from multiple perspectives is an important skill in today's society. In the content areas, students are often expected to examine a topic and be able to identify both the positive side as well as the drawbacks of an issue. Helping students refine this skill can be accomplished in many curriculum areas.

A two-column plus/minus chart allows students to record the pros and the cons of an issue. Under the plus sign the student records the pros, and under the minus column the cons.

See Plus/Minus (page 100).

In a math class, if a student is asked to consider the pros and cons of a particular strategy for problem solving (e.g., guess and check) he/she could record this information under the two columns.

Guess and Check as a problem solving strategy	
+	**—**
Easy — everyone can try it. Usually ends up in finding an answer Can try this if you don't know what else to do.	May take a long time. May not result in an answer. May not understand the math or the reason for the answer.

If the student wishes to make a decision or compare options, the chart simply needs to be extended and a weighting system used.

See Pro/Con (page 101).

Should I smoke					
Option	PRO	Pts.	CON	Pts.
Yes	Will fit in	5	Costs a lot of money	5
	Look older	3	Parents will be angry	3
			Bad for my health	5
			Clothes stink	3
			Teeth yellow	3
		(8)		(19)

If students are trying to decide how to handle peer pressure to use drugs, the options can be listed in the first column and the pros and cons recorded for each option in the second and third columns. Next the student needs to consider that a simple tally may not help them make the best decision, as some pros and cons have a greater importance or a bigger impact. For each pro and each con the student should give an importance/impact score from one to five. Those with the most importance/impact receive a score of five, and those with the least, a one. Then the student can compare the options based on the total points associated with each.

Options for handling Peer pressure				
Option	PRO	Pts.	CON	Pts.
Give in	People like you	5	May get in trouble	4
		3	Feel bad/guilty later	4
			May be in danger	5
(−11)			Harder to stand up to them later	3
		(5)		(16)
Make an excuse or walk away	Removed from situation	4	May make fun of you	4
	Don't look bad	5	Won't work every time	3
	Don't get into trouble	4		
(+ 6)		(13)		(7)
Stand firm	Means you're strong	4	May make fun of you	4
	Feel good about self	4	Won't be your friend	5
	Don't get in trouble	4		
(+3)		(12)		(9)

Point and Counterpoint

See Point and Counterpoint (page 102).

As well as teaching students how to look at two sides of one issue, we can help students respond to an argument or position that is presented to them. Try providing students with a focus question that has opposing viewpoints:

Should Canada sign the Kyoto Accord?
Should marijuana be legalized?
Should the fishery have quotas limiting the amount of fish that can be caught each year?

Have students consider both sides of the issue. Use the Point and Counterpoint template as a framework for a whole-class activity to encourage students to look at two sides of an issue.

1. Students are presented with the focus question (e.g., Should marijuana be legalized?).
2. The class is asked to vote, with a show of hands, their position on this topic—yes or no.
3. Students are divided into the small groups according to a common position. Each group is given two copies of the Point and Counterpoint chart.
4. Beginning with the position they did not vote for, each group is each asked to record, on sticky notes, points or arguments that they anticipate the opposing groups will use in trying to support their point of view. These are placed in the Point column on the first chart.
5. The group discusses each of the points that has been made and suggests a counter-point for each one; in other words, how will they argue against it? Each counterpoint can be recorded on a sticky notes and placed across from the corresponding point.
6. Using the second copy of the chart, the group records points in favor of their own position.
7. The group needs to consider counterpoints that may be raised by the other group. Using the notes constructed on the second chart, ask each group to identify one or two points to share with the opposing group. Each group should try to select a point that supports their position and they feel can not easily be challenged.
8. As an entire class, the groups take turns sharing their points and respective counter-points. In an effort to ensure that the discussion goes smoothly, consider establishing rules or expectations ahead of time regarding the process and limits.

Similarity and Difference

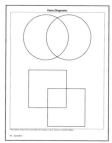

See Venn Diagrams (page 84).

One of the most common ways to encourage students to discuss similarity and difference is using a Venn diagram. The centre shared area is where students record information that is true to both items being discussed. Each of the exterior areas represents the information that is unique to the individual items.

Once students have recorded information in the appropriate place, they can consider the kinds of words that are used to show similarity and difference. Information that is in the centre shows similarity, and this can be communicated using words such as *just as, similarly, like,* etc. Information in the outside areas shows difference, and would use words such as *unlike, whereas, on the other hand, instead of,* etc. Ask students to use this kind of language and vocabulary to describe the relationship between the two ideas being compared.

Metaphors and Analogies

Metaphors and analogies are comparisons that involve a higher level of thinking and understanding. If students are to be successful in constructing metaphors and analogies, they must first have a solid understanding of the subject matter being studied.

Metaphors show a comparison between two ideas. One is compared to the other based on shared characteristics.

> The human heart is a water pump.
>
> For this metaphor, the student explains that both the human heart and a water pump provide the force needed to move a fluid (blood and water) though a series of tubes (veins and pipes) in order to get the fluid where it is needed (the body and the car's radiator).

To help students practise creating metaphors, provide them with some ready-made comparisons and ask them to discuss or explain the metaphor. Ultimately, it is hoped that students will be able to construct their own metaphors to demonstrate their understanding of a concept.

An analogy takes this idea one step farther, showing a relationship between relationships.

> The sun is to the Earth as a Bunsen burner is to a distillation apparatus.
>
> In this analogy, the students must understand three things: the relationship between the sun and the Earth; the relationship between the Bunsen burner and a distillation apparatus; and the similarity between both of these ideas.

1. To help students develop the concept of analogies, give them some examples and ask them to describe or support the analogy based on their knowledge.
2. Next try giving students incomplete analogies and ask them to fill in the blank before justifying.
3. Finally, ask students to construct their own analogies to demonstrate understanding of topics being studied.

Using the Comparison Matrix

See Writing Matrix (page 95).

The same matrix that was used to write the Informational report (see page 40) can be used to help students organize a comparative essay.

1. Identify a research question.
2. Select ideas for comparison. Record these along the top row in cells 2, 3, 4.
3. Decide on criteria for comparison. Record in the first column in cells 5, 9, 13.
4. Record factual information in each of cells 6, 7, 8; 10, 11, 12; 14, 15, 16.
5. Record a summary statement in cell 17.
6. Use the outline to transform the information into a series of cohesive paragraphs. Each horizontal row becomes a paragraph.
   Paragraph 1: Introduction
   • lead sentence: cell 1
   • paragraph sentences: cells 5, 9, 13.
   Paragraph 2: First Criteria
   • lead sentence: cell 5
   • paragraph sentences: cells 6, 7, 8
   Paragraph 3: Second Criteria
   • lead sentence: cell 9

- paragraph sentences: cells 10, 11, 12

Paragraph 4: Third Criteria
- lead sentence: cell 13
- paragraph sentences: cells 14, 15, 16

Paragraph 5: Conclusion
- cell 17

See the chart on page 32 for the sample of comparative writing based on the matrix below.

1 Which kind of fast food is best ?			
Things to compare → Criteria	2 Burgers	3 Pizza	4 Subs
5 Taste	6 • burgers are standard • burgers are pre-made	7 • pizzas made to order • customer can choose toppings	8 • subs are made to order • sub is made in front of customer • sub can be customized to individual taste
9 Variety	10 • variety limited to size/ number of patties • few basic toppings	11 • choice of toppings • basic pizza is standard: dough with sauce and a combination of meat and vegetables	12 • choice of type of bread • can choose main filling • choice of toppings and sauces
13 Price	14 • basic burger costs about a dollar	15 • small pizza costs $5 to $10 • slices are cheaper, but you don't get the same quality or choice	16 • not as cheap as burgers; less expensive than pizza • often there are "club" points so that you can get a free sub
17 The best bet is the sub.			

Personal Writing: Sharing Thoughts, Ideas, and Reactions

Although we often focus our attention to writing that will be made public, it is also important to support students in developing the necessary skills for writing that is more private. Instruction and opportunity for personal response are essential. This kind of writing provides students with the opportunity to reflect on their thinking, synthesize ideas, and document information that they may use at a later date.

Some teachers see personal writing as a way to get to better know a student as a person and as a learner, so the focus is less on the curriculum or what has been learned. Others prefer to use journals as a way to document or record understanding related to the curriculum and the topics studied.

When it comes to assessing personal writing, consider reading and responding to the students' writing without assigning a grade. If a grade is necessary, try documenting the work as *Complete* or *Incomplete*. Because it is personal writing, it may not be completely shared with others (including you).

Learning Logs

Learning logs are a great way for students to document their learning. Instead of recording notes or information that the teacher has provided, a log can be used to record what the student understands as a result of what is learned in and out of school. The log becomes a written record of a student's thinking and may include a variety of information.

Across the Curriculum

Possible topics for logs in all subjects include

- personal accounts describing students' experiences
- understandings or information students believe to be true
- questions
- sketches and drawings
- connections to other ideas
- reaction, feeling/emotions

Learning logs don't have to be fancy. In order for logs to be effective, however, students should have a designated log that they can keep on hand at all times and can easily locate. A learning log can simply be

- a section in a student's binder, or notebook. Make sure it is clearly marked.
- a small notebook
- a small notebook cut in half
- custom pages stapled together as a booklet or stapled inside a file folder. Custom pages may include a blank area for sketches, lines for printed text, and prompts for reflection and writing.
- an electronic file

New–Now–Next Journals

See the New–Now–Next Journal (page 103).

The New–Now–Next Journal allows students to document their learning. Each week students are expected to reflect on their learning and make some notes in their journals.

Column one, New, is where the student records what has been learned during the week. This can be a skill the student has mastered (e.g., using a beam balance, using a microscope, multiplying positive and negative integers, using a gazetteer to locate places in an atlas) or knowledge acquired (e.g., causes of WWI, components of a balanced diet, the difference between linear and nonlinear relationships).

Column two, Now, is where the student comments or expresses how he/she is now feeling about the class and/or activities that took place during the current week. The student may choose to comment on one or more of the following:

- what she/he enjoyed
- what he/she found difficult
- suggestions she/he has for the future

The third and final column, Next, is where the student identifies one goal for the week ahead, something he/she would like to work on, or improve.

Me & You Journal

See Me & You Journal (page 104).

A less-structured journal is a Me & You Journal. This is a simple way to get students to share their thinking without too many rules. These journals provide a space for students to write a couple of sentences each day.

The first column is the date. In the second column, the student shares something about learning, school, etc., and gives feedback on how he/she found the last class. Students who feel good about the class and their contribution would circle the thumbs-up symbol. For a class a student found confusing or that caused them difficulty, the thumbs-down symbol would be circled. The thumb to the side is for those who might be unsure about some of the material or felt they didn't participate a lot, but weren't disruptive.

The third column is for the teacher's response. Limited space is provided so that the teacher's feedback does not overwhelm students. Some of the topics that students may write about include

- questions about information presented in class
- something they learned or liked about class
- things that are happening at home or with friends
- an idea for an assignment or project
- something they find difficult to understand

4-Square Log

The 4-Square Log offers students the opportunity to include visual text as part of their personal writing. This is particularly helpful in subjects such as science and math, where students may have difficulty explaining an idea or concept just with words.

- The student records any key words that are part of the unit of study in the top left box.

See 4-Square Log (page 105).

- In the top right box go sentences or phrases that describe new information or understandings.
- The bottom right box is for questions the student has.
- In the bottom left box the student may draw a picture or a visual to help explain the topic or concept.

Course: *Math*	Date: *Feb. 18*
Key Words *equilateral* *isosceles* *scalene* *right angle* *interior angle*	Ideas & New Information *Equilateral triangles have 3 equal sides with 3 equal interior angles.* *An isosceles triangle has 2 equal sides.* *All 3 sides and interior angles are different on a scalene triangle.* *A right angle is 90°.*
Picture or Visual *scalene* *equilateral* *isosceles*	Questions I Still Have *Can you ever have an isosceles triangle with a right angle?*

Journal Prompts

Teachers can support and encourage students' reflective writing by providing them with prompts or stems to focus their reflection. Some prompts that prompt thinking include

- The most important thing I learned was...
- The most interesting thing I learned was....
- Questions that continue to bug me are...
- A connection that I made was...
- This reminds me of...
- _____ is kind of like this because....
- Another way to do this is...
- A message I have for others is....
- An alternative to this is...
- I can apply this to the real world by ....
- If we had known this it would have changed...
- This knowledge affects my life...
- I believe...

Poetry: A Way of Knowing

Word Wise

acrostic
free verse
pyramid
concrete
voices

Poetry is a form of writing that can be effectively used in content areas. Because poetry is about creating mental images through words and expressing a concept or idea as succinctly as possible, it requires students to communicate their understanding. Content teachers can give students the option of using poetry as a form of communication.

Poetry can be fun. It can also be a challenge to do in a way that both is meaningful for the student and meets curriculum outcomes. Below are suggestions for more effective use of poetry:

- read aloud poems (particular to your content area) to the class
- discuss poems and their meaning (general discussion, not a line-by-line analysis)
- emphasize that not all poetry rhymes
- discuss the importance of choosing the best word, not the one that rhymes
- set a purpose for the writing; what do you hope to accomplish?
- model a couple of approaches to writing poetry

Forms of Poetry

There are many different forms of poetry.

Acrostic

Acrostic poems are popular because students perceive this kind of poetry as easy. The challenge is to encourage students to choose words and phrases that effectively communicate the idea or concept. The letters of a chosen word are written down the left-hand side of the page. Each letter from the original word then becomes the first letter of another word or phrase that describes or relates to the main word. A more challenging approach to the acrostic poem is to try to link or weave each of the lines together in proper syntax while maintaining flow.

Earth
Natural and
Vibrant
Indescribable beauty, but
Resources are
Overextended and overused
Needing protection from
Man's actions and our
Excessive energy consumption
Needless harvesting now
Taking its toll

Free Verse

Free verse is really flexible poetry. The only rule for free verse is that it has no rules. Free verse may describe something or tell a story. When writing free verse, careful attention must be paid to the ideas you wish to communicate, word choice, and organization. One way of writing free verse is to begin with an existing paragraph, pull out the most essential words and ideas, and build on these. Another approach is to brainstorm a list of descriptive words and then organize them so that powerful images are created.

Rollercoaster
Up and up the track
pulled by chains
energy is being stored.
Higher
and higher
more and more potential.
Teetering on the top
maximum potential
maximum anticipation.
Suddenly plunging
gravity pulling you to the ground
potential is now kinetic
moving fast, and faster, and fastest
until we hit bottom.
The ride continues.

Pyramid Poems

Pyramid poems provide the student who needs structure with a framework. A pyramid poem is structured in the shape of a pyramid, and contains five lines. The first line consists of one word, the second has two words, the third has three words, and so on. The teacher can decide what kind of information should be recorded on each line. A possible framework is this:

1. The first line is the object or topic being described.
2. The second is adjectives that describe the object.
3. Third is actions or verbs.
4. Fourth provides an antonym, or opposite
5. The last line is a comparison or something that is similar.

Bullies
Tough, mean
Taunt and intimidate
Never kind or compassionate
Like bulldozers destroying fragile land

Concrete Poetry

This type of poetry is arranged on the page in the shape of the subject that is being written about. A poem about a sphere would be arranged in a circular shape; a poem about a tornado or lightning could be arranged like a tornado or a lightning bolt.

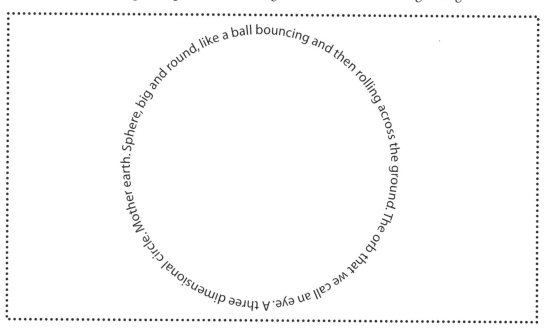

Across the Curriculum

If the student wants to write poetry about a number of weather-related topics, he/she may choose to write smaller poems that, when combined, create an entire picture (e.g., clouds, lightning, raindrops, wind, ground)

Poems for Two Voices

This kind of poetry is great for a topic that has two perspectives or points of view, and can emphasize comparison, or similarity and difference. The poem is arranged in a form similar to a Venn diagram. One perspective is recorded on the left, the other on the right. In the centre are any lines that are common or shared between the two. When poems for two voices are read aloud, each person reads one of the outer columns; the centre is read by both readers in unison.

Sent Away

Lost and alone.
Sent away

To Reservations,
Undesirable lands,
Residential schools.

Sent away

To France,
The Southern States,
Far away French colonies

Sent away.

Guilty of being different.

Native

French

A different color skin.

A different language.

A different way of life.

A different religion.

Not like those laying claim
to our land.

A land we loved.

A land we worked.

A land that we were part of.

A land we called our home.

Only wanting to live our
lives, as we have for

thousands of years

hundreds of years

The history books, they call
it

relocation

expulsion

Two events

different time and place

same outcome

History repeats itself

Across the Curriculum

Social studies and PDR are areas that often require a student to look at an issue from multiple points of view. Poems for two voices can be useful in these content areas.

Posters: Creating Visual Texts

<table>
<tr><td>

Word Wise

visuals
persuade
inform
space
size
color

</td></tr>
</table>

How many times have you given students the opportunity to demonstrate their understanding of a topic in a visual way and were disappointed? Too many! Many students will choose to create a poster because they perceive it to be less work or easier than writing an essay or a report. Creating a quality poster can take just as much, if not more, effort as a written piece. Unfortunately, if students receive little or no guidance or direction in how to create an effective poster, the end result may lack the impact you and the student were hoping for. Below are some activities to consider when teaching students about posters as a means of communication.

What's the Purpose?

It always comes back to purpose. Before students can begin creating a poster, they need to clearly understand what they are hoping to accomplish. Many posters fall into one of two categories:

- Posters that promote or persuade
- Posters that provide information

Posters that are persuasive in nature attempt to convince you or sway your opinion. Advertising, political, or social campaigns all fit this category. These posters want you to buy a product or buy into a belief.

Posters may also be informative, simply providing information about a particular topic. Posters in subway, bus, or train stations provide directions or information about the location and times for these modes of transportation. A poster about a bird, such as the chimney swift, may give information about the bird, its life, and where it can be found.

What you are hoping to accomplish will have a huge impact on how you go about creating your poster. Provide students with sample posters and ask them to sort them into the two categories.

Elements of an Effective Poster

Essential and effective information: No matter how flashy and creative your poster is, it must contain information that is of interest or is necessary to the audience. Unnecessary or unrelated information makes it more difficult to achieve your purpose, as it can confuse your reader. As important as including only the most essential information is that the information provided be accurate and correct. Information that is incomplete makes it more difficult to understand your poster. Incorrect information may mislead or misrepresent, and is not acceptable for something that is being published or shared with others. Make sure your information is effective when it comes to getting your message across.

Organization of information: In print text, information is organized from left to right, top to bottom. The information on posters can also flow in this general direction. It is also common, however, to place the central or main idea in the centre of the poster with supporting information surrounding it. This organization works best when there is one central focus that is significantly more important than other information, so the central position emphasizes its importance.

Use of space: Use of space includes how you lay out the information on the entire page. A good poster uses all the space available. Posters with the information crammed into one section are hard to read and unappealing. Borders and white space help to frame the poster. Text should be spaced well enough to be easy to read. Single spacing is too close; try one-and-a-half or double spacing.

Size: The size of the print and visual information is an essential part of a poster. Posters are meant to be read from a distance, so the information must be presented in such a way that this is possible. Not all information is equally important and cannot all be of the same size. Titles and subtitles should be larger in size than body text. Deciding on size means planning your poster in advance, including making decisions about what is most important. Also remember that sometimes small is the way to go. Just ask anyone what the term "fine print" refers to and they will certainly show an understanding of the use of small fonts.

Use of color: Color is an important aspect in any visual. Some things to consider when choosing color:

- Choose colors that help to convey your message. Black and white may be effective choices if your topic is pollution and you want to convey the idea of something dark and dreary. A poster about Italy may incorporate the national colors of red and green. Something about conservation may incorporate lots of blue and green, which are associated with a clean and healthy environment.
- A single color stands out. If the text of your poster is in black, using another color for selected words can draw attention to these words.
- Too much color can be distracting. The message of the poster can be lost in the competing color scheme. Use a large palate of colors only if it helps to accomplish your purpose.
- Primary and complementary colors are easy to see and work well together. Primary colors are red, yellow, and blue. Complementary colors are the combinations of primary colors: red and yellow (orange), yellow and blue (green), and blue and red (purple).
- Consider color as a background. Using colored pieces of paper to create a background is an effective way of including color. If a border is desired, simply place a different colored paper of a smaller size on top of the color paper.

Use of visuals: Visuals are important parts of a poster. The job of a visual is to communicate an idea not appearing in print, or to add meaning to the print. Common and well-known symbols can be used to represent an idea instead of explaining the idea in words. The Canadian flag, a peace symbol, a dollar sign, and the symbol for recycling each communicate an idea, requiring little or no addition explanation. Other visuals such as graphs, maps, and charts may also speak for themselves, but often are included to provide supporting information. On a poster, the visuals should be clear in their composition and their message.

Poster Presentation Points

*See Poster
Presentation Points
(page 106).*

Organization

- Move from left to right, top to bottom.
- Place the main idea in the centre.
- Create a pattern that is easy for the eye to follow.

Space

- Use all of the space—don't cram.
- Balance the borders and white space.
- Space the print so it is easy to read.

Size

- Size is important—can you read the poster from a distance?
- Greater importance requires greater size (e.g., headings vs subheadings).
- Use a larger size to make things stand out.

Color

- Choose colors that are associated with your topic.
- Use color in borders, visuals, and words.
- Have a reason for every color you use.
- Sometimes less is more; too much color can be distracting.

Visuals

- Include symbols, charts, graphs, maps, photos, diagrams, tables, illustrations, etc.
- Use visuals to communicate ideas instead of the print.
- Use visuals to add meaning to the print.
- Clarity is key.

WWE

*See WWE template
(page 107).*

One of the best ways to help students understand the anatomy of a poster is to show them as many different kinds of posters as possible. Rather than simply having them look at the posters and identify the characteristics and techniques used, have the students go one step further. The chart on page 107 prompts students to examine a poster and identify what the author has done in terms of elements of the poster: Purpose, Information, Organization, Space, Size, Color, Visuals. In the second column students explain why the author chose to use that feature. Finally, the student should give their own evaluation of the effectiveness of this aspect of the poster.

Pamphlets, Folders, and 3D Models: Other Ways to Present Information

Word Wise

landscape
portrait
pamphlet
folder
accordion
silhouette
3D
mobile
minibook

While posters may be a popular way to represent information visually, there are many other options. This section will highlight just a few ways that students can present their information in a visual and effective manner.

The key to using a variety of presentation models is to ensure that the students are given the level of support necessary to be successful:

- Model techniques for physically making the pamphlet, book, model, etc.
- Explain your expectations in terms of level of detail required.
- Provide models that show the quality you are expecting.
- Build a rubric or a target for assessment.

Pamphlets

Pamphlets are a method of presentation that may appear to be easy, but require advanced planning, organization, and knowledge of the subject matter in order to be effective. Pamphlets can be laid out in a variety of ways. Two basic types of pamphlets are

- bi-fold: page is folded in half
- tri-fold: page is folded into thirds

Regardless of the format used, there are a number of considerations when constructing a pamphlet:

- headings should have a larger font than the body text
- pictures are helpful to the reader
- bullets work well to explain quick facts or highlight a list
- borders help to frame the work and make it easier to read
- the first page may act as a cover, with a title and contact information
- the inside pages should contain the most important information with less important information being placed at the back.

Folders

Folders are similar to pamphlets, in that they provide the writer with the option of a cover. To make a folder,

1. Begin with heavier paper folded in half. This will be the front and back cover.
2. Fold a plain sheet of paper in half. This will be the inside where the text is written.
3. Cut the inside paper so it is slightly smaller than the cover.
4. Record your text on one side of the plain sheet of paper and decorate the cover.
5. Glue the blank side of the paper to the inside of the cover. This keeps pages from being loose, and it also creates the effect of a border.

Accordion Books

Accordion books can be made by simply folding a long piece of paper towards alternating sides.

1. Begin with a piece of paper that is longer than it is wide (4 to 6 times longer than its width). You may cut this from a large piece of paper, or take two or three pieces of construction paper, cut them in half the long way, and tape the pieces end to end.
2. Fold the long piece of paper in half.
3. Fold each section in half again.
4. Continue until you have pages the size you desire.
5. Alternate the folds so they fold to the front and then to the back, creating an accordian fold.
6. Crease the edges.
7. Cut pieces of white paper that are 2–3 cm smaller (in length and width) than construction paper, glue one on each page so the construction paper acts as a border.

Silhouettes and Shapes

Silhouettes and shapes can be used to present information in a very visual manner. Writing is presented on a piece of paper that is cut in the shape of the topic. Or cut several blank pieces of paper in the same shape and create a book, using the heavier paper as front and back covers.

3D: Boxes, Pyramids, and Mobiles

Information can be presented in multiple ways using three-dimensional objects. Possibilities include the following:

- Build a six-sided cube and record information on each of the sides. This works well when trying to show multiple dimensions or perspectives of a single topic.
- Build a pyramid and record information on each of the sides. This is effective when trying to show a hierarchy.
- Create a mobile with objects/papers that hang from a frame. Each of the hanging objects can have information recorded that provides additional information about the main idea.

Minibooks

Minibooks can be made by folding and cutting a single piece of paper or pieces of paper to create a small book.

PART 3

Providing Feedback

One of the most important things we can do as teachers is provide students with quality feedback about their learning. This includes sharing with them their successes and strengths, as well as pointing out areas of need. It is important, however, that when pointing out areas for improvement we don't stop with simple identification. Students require concrete feedback that tells them what they need to improve and points them in the right direction when it comes to making these improvements.

In this part you will find key words, practical strategies, and ideas organized around innovative ways to incorporate feedback into your classroom instruction.

Providing Specific Feedback
Profile for Nonfiction Writing: Checklists and Rubrics
Publishing Conference
PentaRep: Multiple Representations of Understanding
Portfolios
Promoting Positive Writing

Providing Specific Feedback

Word Wise

specific
criteria
target

Throughout the day, teachers make hundreds of comments to students about their work and their learning. It is important that you try to make these comments as specific as possible. Think about how ineffective a comment like "good work" or "try harder" is to a student. The first example may make students feel good about themselves, but it doesn't support them in knowing what to repeat or change for the future.

Below are some examples of comments that are specific and can be helpful to students. The first comment of each pair focuses on something the student did well; the second makes a suggestion that would help to improve the writing. It is important, for both kinds of comment, to provide information that is as specific as possible. Also, it is not necessary for comments always to be put in writing. Comments can be effective if shared orally, especially if it is done by referring to a student's actual work.

Topic/Aspect	Sample Comments
strong **ideas**	• Information is accurate and well researched. • Ideas are vague and require more detail. Consider giving examples to help strengthen the message.
good **organization**	• The writing is well organized. The piece has a clear beginning, middle, and end. • The sequence of ideas is confusing. Try using a numbered list or transition words such as *first*, *second*, *next*, and *finally* to improve the organization.
effective **word choice**	• The key words and technical terms are used correctly. • In your persuasive writing, try to include language that is stronger or more convincing. Think about using words like *must*, *it is essential*, *experts say*, *in my own experience*, etc.
standard **conventions**	• Use of end punctuation (period, question mark, exclamation mark) is good. Remember, when using quotation marks, to insert a comma prior to the beginning of the quote and to use a capital letter for the first word inside the quote. • Spelling of key terms is weak. Refer back to source, or use a dictionary to make corrections.
effective **sentences**	• Writing effectively combines some short and some long sentences to make it more interesting to read. • Most sentences begin the same way. Try to change or vary the words you use at the beginning of the sentence.

Making Feedback Visible: Target

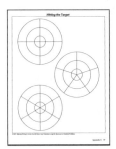

See Hitting the Target (page 97).

When an oral comment is not enough and you want students to have something on paper to reflect on, there are a number of options available. One method is to simply put into writing what you would tell a student in conversation. This is good for students who are strong when it comes to reading and interpreting print text. Another option is to provide students with a visual representation of feedback.

A target simply breaks down for students the expectations for a piece of work. Expectations are assigned to sections of the target prior to completion of the work. As they progress through the writing, students can continually refer to the target as a reminder of what the criteria is for success. Following completion, the student, his/her peers, or the teacher can assess the quality of the work and indicate how close the student was to hitting the target by using shading on the target. For example, if the student did an excellent or very good job on one of the criteria, the portion of the target closest to the centre would be shaded in; criteria not reached would be represented by shading in the outermost ring.

If the student was working on a poster that demonstrated the use of measurement in everyday situations, the following criteria might be established:

Minimum of 10 measurements are represented.

Minimum of 3 measurements are represented.

Situation is realistic.

Information is accurate.

Use of space, color, and visuals contribute to the message.

Making Feedback Visible: From Here to There

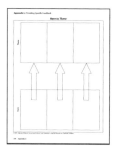

See Here to There (page 108).

The Here to There visual is another way to provide feedback to students about their learning. It offers feedback to the student in a manner that is similar to the Target, but with an additional layer—suggestions for the future.

Teacher and students brainstorm a list of criteria for the piece of writing. These are recorded in the right column. Next they identify what There looks like, including a brief description of what a successful piece of writing would include. In other words, if they are aiming for success, what will they see when they get there?

After students have completed the writing, they can self-assess where they think they are in relation to the end goal, where they are trying to get. This is recorded in the Here column. The centre area, inside the block arrow, can be partly or wholly shaded in by the student or teacher to indicate how close the student is to reaching the goal. This is also a place for the student and teacher to record one or two concrete suggestions for how the student can get from where they are with this piece of work to their end goal, specifically what they can do to improve the piece of writing.

Assignment: Lab Report

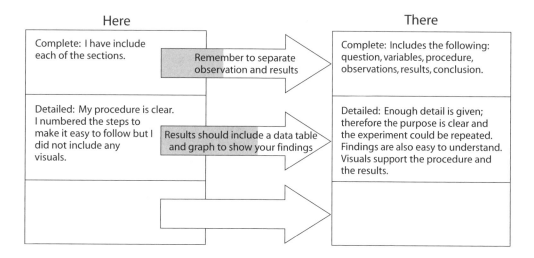

Profile for Nonfiction Writing: Checklists and Rubrics

Word Wise

checklist
rubric
organization
ideas
engagement
conventions

Checklists and rubrics are effective ways to provide feedback to students about their learning. Both checklists and rubrics outline the criteria or expectations for a particular piece of work. For both forms, the key is to create them with students or, at the very least, to provide students with them prior to the work that they do.

Appendix M provides some checklists that can be used by students and teachers when assessing specific pieces of writing, as well as a generic rubric that can be used with almost any text that a student creates. For information about checklists and rubrics specific to portfolios, see pages 78–79.

Checklists

See Checklists for Informational Writing (page 110), Persuasive Writing (page 111), Procedural Writing (page 112), and Comparative Writing (page 113).

Part 2 of this book provided an overview of a variety of text patterns. Each kind of text has its own conventions; therefore, when it comes to assessment and providing feedback to students, there are particular things that one looks for in each type of writing. When constructing a checklist consider the following:

- What is the purpose of the writing?
- What is the structure or pattern of the writing?
- Are there basic expectations with regard to conventions, neatness, and presentation?
- How important is accuracy of information?
- What concepts should be explained?

Use the Checklist template on page 109 to construct your own checklists with students. The checklists on pages 110 to 113 can be used by students to reflect on various kinds of writing. As students become more familiar with each kind of writing, encourage them to add to the list of criteria

Rubrics

See Sample Rubric (page 114).

The rubric provides a basic framework for nonfiction writing. Shared with students before they write, it can serve as a guide and provide direction. Created with or by students prior to writing, it is even more effective in helping them internalize the expectations and qualities of good writing.

The rubric on page 114 is general enough that it can be used with most writing tasks. Whether for a lab report, an information report, poetry, or a poster, it allows careful consideration of a student's work.

Publishing Conference

Conferring with students to review their writing is an important part of helping students develop as writers and, perhaps more importantly, as learners. It allows the teacher to gain insight into a student's thinking, and to see how his/her writing is conveying this understanding. A student conference can be very informal—a quick conversation with the student at his/her desk—or a more formal, possibly scheduled conversation that lasts for 5 to 15 minutes.

Managing Conversations

It is important not to feel so overwhelmed by the management of conversations with students that you choose not to engage in them at all. Keep in mind the importance of quality conversations. This means knowing what you want to discuss with the student, structuring the conversation so it highlights strengths and needs, and ensuring the student has the opportunity to share their own observations, ideas, and questions.

These tips may make conversations more manageable and more productive:

- Try to have a one-on-one conversation (even a short one) with at least one student each period.
- Have one thing to discuss prepared ahead of time.
- Whenever possible, have a piece of student work or another writing sample on hand to discuss and highlight.
- Always highlight a strength.
- Always discuss an area of need; be as specific as possible with suggestions.
- Limit the number of things that are discussed: focus on one or two areas and have the student work on these before moving on to other areas. Too much feedback can be overwhelming.
- Look for opportunities to have conversations when the whole group is working independently.
- If two or more students could benefit from the same conversation, pull a small group together for a discussion.
- Following your conversations, record a brief note that you can refer to later: sticky notes work well for this, as do index cards (one card per student). Include the date and one or two things that were discussed.
- Invite the student to share their observations, comments, and questions.
- Vary the location of conversations: go to your students, have them come to you, or find a quiet place in the room.
- Insist on no interruptions when you are speaking with individual students. This needs to be modeled and reinforced from day one.

Encouraging Effective Editing

If a student's writing is going to be published, it is necessary that it include standard conventions of spelling, punctuation, grammar, etc. Sometimes it can be a challenge to give students specific feedback about the conventions or mechanics of their writing without taking over and making all the changes for them. Using page protectors allows the teacher and student to discuss and make necessary changes together, lets the student make the changes independently, and then allows the student to check work against the teacher/student recommendations.

1. Before discussing the work, the teacher places the piece of writing in a plastic page protector, or covers it with a transparency and secure it with a paperclip.
2. The teacher asks the student to point out any words he/she thinks are misspelled. Using an overhead marker, the student circles these words on the plastic covering.
3. Next, using a different color, the teacher circles or identifies additional misspelled words.
4. The teacher and student can then discuss the correct spelling and make changes on the page protector/transparency. The student is able to see where changes need to be made and what these changes look like, but the actual piece of work has not been altered.
5. When the discussion is over, the teacher can decide to let the student have the page protector/transparency, or to keep it and ask the student to make the changes on his/her own, having had the benefit of the discussion.
6. Once corrections have been made, the student can either bring the piece to the teacher or use the plastic sleeve/transparency themselves to check their work. By placing the sleeve/transparency with the correct spellings over the piece of work, the student and teacher can see which changes were successfully made and where any problems continue.

See Editors' Marks chart (page 115).

This same strategy can be used to edit a piece of writing for more that just spelling. Changes can also be recommended for conventions including

- use of capital letters
- punctuation
- sentence structure
- organization
- paragraphing

Remember, however, that a student can focus on only a few things at any one time. A student may be overwhelmed and may not learn from the experience if expected to correct all editing errors at once. Try to focus on one or two things at a time.

Across the Curriculum

One thing that can help make editing more efficient is the use of a standard set of editors' marks. Their use is most effective if they are used in all subjects and, if possible, across grade levels. The chart on page 115 shows a suggested list. See if your school, or at least your grade level, can agree on a set of common marks.

PentaRep: Multiple Representations of Understanding

Writing as a means of communicating understanding poses a challenge for some learners. This is especially true if the options for communication are limited or narrow. One of your roles is to provide feedback about what the students have learned, and also to offer feedback related to how they are demonstrating this learning.

First, take a closer look at five ways students can and should be able to use to demonstrate their conceptual understanding of a topic: concrete, symbolic, pictorial, verbal, and contextual. The pentagram below provides a visual that briefly explains the five representations, and highlights the role of writing.

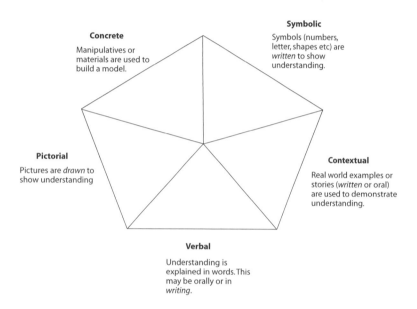

Concrete

Manipulatives or materials are used to build a model.

Symbolic

Symbols (numbers, letter, shapes etc) are *written* to show understanding.

Pictorial

Pictures are *drawn* to show understanding

Contextual

Real world examples or stories (*written* or oral) are used to demonstrate understanding.

Verbal

Understanding is explained in words. This may be orally or in *writing*.

Using PentaRep

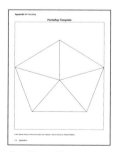

See PentaRep Template (page 116).

Once you understand the pentagram symbol and the five representations, the PentaRep form can become an assessment tool for teachers and students.

Program Assessment

Teachers can use the PentaRep as a quick way to assess the overall program and the opportunities students have, or the expectations teachers have for students to represent their understanding in all five ways.

1. Plan your instruction.
2. Highlight the representations modeled and expected from students as part of the instruction.
3. Shade in the corresponding portion of the pentagram.
4. Review the PentaRep at the end of a month or term. If there is one section with little or no shading, this may be an area that needs attention.

Student Assessment

Students can use the PentaRep to self-assess their learning and/or learning style, by doing the following:

1. Place a copy of the PentaRep in your portfolio or journal.
2. Find samples of work that demonstrate understanding. Identify the particular representation used in communicating understanding
3. Shade in the corresponding section of the pentagram, or record the title of the piece of work there.
4. Look for a balance of representations. What does this tell you about yourself as a learner?

Across the Curriculum

While these particular five representations originated in mathematics, they can be relevant and valuable across all subject areas. Subjects such as science, social studies, and health benefit when students have the opportunity to learn and express their understanding concretely, pictorially, verbally, and contextually. Below are some examples that apply to a variety of subjects.

Concrete
- Build a model
- Demonstrate an idea
- Create an invention

Pictorial
- Draw a picture
- Create a poster
- Create a mind map

Verbal
- Explain or describe understanding
- Present a skit
- Give an oral presentation
- Create a piece of writing

Symbolic
- Show as an equation

Contextual
- Give a real world example
- Incorporate into a story

PentaRep as an Instructional Tool

Use PentaRep Template on page 116 in Appendix O. Give students a problem to solve, then use the pentagram as a spinner to determine the method or representation students will use to demonstrate their understanding.

1. Place a paperclip on the centre of the pentagram.
2. Place a pencil inside one end of the paperclip.
3. Spin the paperclip, and wait for it to point to one of the five representations.
4. Solve the math problem and share the solution using the representation identified on the spinner.

Portfolios

Word Wise
learning portfolio
outcome
reflection

Ask artists, carpenters, teachers, architects, graphic designers, writers, etc. to demonstrate or reflect on their achievements, and many will share a portfolio of their work. Portfolios can also be very useful when it comes to assessment of student learning. English teachers have long used writing portfolios for assessment purposes. Because much of the work we have students do in the content areas is communicated through writing, or the creation of a text, it makes sense for content teachers also to have students keep writing portfolios. In the case of the content-area class, the emphasis may not be on the writing as much as it is on the learning. For this reason I will refer to these portfolios as learning portfolios. While the focus will be slightly different, the process and structure may be quite similar.

In content-area classes, it is the "what" or the substance of the portfolio that matters. This shift in focus from form to substance parallels the shift from a writing portfolio in an English class to a learning portfolio in the content-area class. In an English class the focus may be more heavily on how ideas are communicated, and the range and quality of the writing. In the content area, the focus is on the concepts and the learning. The writing is important in that it is through writing that the student is able to demonstrate understanding.

With this in mind, it is important to expand the notion of a portfolio so it is inclusive of all learning. Some portfolios are simply collections of the students' best work. These "good binders" show what the student has achieved, but miss the opportunity to showcase the learning process and the growth that comes from struggle and failure. A portfolio can have a very broad scope. It may include

- samples of the student's best work
- rough notes that show understanding or an idea
- something the student found difficult
- something the student enjoyed
- two pieces of work that show growth or improvement from one to the next
- work that shows depth of understanding of a concept

A learning portfolio can be organized in a variety of ways. One common method of organization is to have students collect samples of work and place these in a binder or folder. With the growth of technology, many students are now using the computer or digital camera to put together a portfolio: the portfolio can be completely electronic. Perhaps the student creates his/her own website, or creates a Powerpoint presentation with photos and links to other pieces of electronic work. It is also possible to have a portfolio that combines the traditional with the electronic. For example, a digital camera can be used to take a photo of a three-dimensional project or a learning experience, and the print copy is then placed in traditional binder portfolio.

If students are making a traditional portfolio, the suggestions below may be helpful:

- Use a binder so work can be securely attached.
- Create dividers to separate units of study.
- Ensure that each unit has a minimum of three pieces of work.

- Include work that shows diversity.
- Show "good" work as well as work that is in progress or work that shows growth and depth of understanding.
- Place work in plastic sleeves so it is neat and protected.
- Include a table of contents.
- Include a reflection for each piece of work.
- Keep a space for assessments and letters/comments from others who have reviewed the portfolio.
- Take time every two weeks to work on the portfolio: selecting work, writing reflections, sharing it with others and getting feedback.

Reflecting on Learning

Anyone can collect a bunch of papers in a binder or folder. It is the reflection process that takes the process of collecting and makes it purposeful and reflective on the learning and achievement. It is also through reflection that future goals can be identified.

Helping the student reflect on concepts and process means ensuring they understand what the intended concepts and process were/are. Each province or state has an identified curriculum. This curriculum articulates the required concepts and knowledge, as well as the required skills and processes. One of the easiest ways to help students understand these requirements is not to give copies of the curriculum guide, but rather to share with them, in a manner they can understand, the key outcomes or standards. This can be done at the beginning of a unit, reinforced daily, and revisited at the end of the unit.

1. List outcomes, in student-friendly language, and post in the classroom.
2. Share outcomes and discuss with students at the beginning of the unit.
3. Each day refer to what the students are doing in relation to the outcomes.
4. At the end of the unit, ask students to select two or three pieces of work that demonstrate success, growth, or future direction in relation to the outcomes.
5. Have students write a short reflection on their learning and place this with the piece of work in their portfolio.

Reflection Cards

See Student Reflection Prompt Cards (page 117).

For many students, knowing how to reflect or deciding what to say is the hardest part. Reflection cards can support students in this process. A reflection card can be a color-coded index card or a square of paper. Reflection cards can be open-ended or provide prompts for the student. The level of support may need to be highest at the beginning of the process, and gradually lessen as the student builds confidence and understands what is expected.

Color-coded index cards are an effective means of encouraging reflection. The use of color-coded cards allows for quick reference and makes gaps visible. Students with only one color of cards attached to pieces of work are demonstrating only one aspect of learning. As they look through the portfolio and see only, say, yellow cards, they know to look for artifacts that represent other areas.

For example, in the science class cards may be assigned as follows:

Yellow = knowledge and concepts

Blue = processes and skills

Green = attitudes

Below are samples of a Grade 8 student's reflection following a unit on cells.

Blue card: *I have selected "Investigating Cells" for my portfolio because it is a piece of my best work. It shows that I know how to make a wet mount slide. I have listed the steps in correct order and have given enough detail that someone else could use these directions to make a wet mount slide. I have also drawn pictures to explain the steps (in case someone couldn't understand the words).*

Yellow card: *I chose this piece of work (Investigating Cells) for my portfolio because it shows that I understand the cell structure of plants. After I made a wet mount slide of the onion skin, I drew and labeled all of the parts of the plant cell.*

Prepared reflection cards with prompts (see page 117) can be helpful. The student chooses a prompt card and then selects a piece of work that best reflects the idea communicated on the card. It is then up to the student to write a more detailed explanation of why they chose that piece of work.

Audience for a Learning Portfolio

See Audience Feedback Prompts (page 118).

Traditionally a portfolio for the English teacher is shared with only the English teacher; work done in social studies class has always stayed in social studies class. Just as looking at the substance of a portfolio is a unconventional task, it is also important to consider unconventional audiences. Perhaps the most ideal situation is one of collaboration. Students could assemble a learning portfolio for a content-area teacher and also have pieces of work from this course count for their English course.

For example, a Grade 7 student compiles a portfolio for social studies. In this portfolio are the following:

- a comparative essay comparing the role of women in the First and Second World War
- a short biography of Nelly McLung
- a poster encouraging people to join the war effort
- a series of letters from a war bride to her family back in England

The social studies teacher can evaluate the portfolio in terms of the student's understanding of the major concepts of the unit. The English teacher could look at these same pieces of work in terms of their composition. With this kind of an approach, teachers are recognizing and valuing all learning; the student sees the interconnectedness of learning and the relationship between subject areas. Such an approach will go a long way towards breaking down the compartmentalization of school and building on the idea of skill transfer.

It is also important to consider potential audiences for a student's work other than teachers. Arranging for students to share their work with other students can be an important part of the learning process. Having students share their work with other adults is also a valuable experience. Just as some students need support when reflecting on their own work, prompt cards can assist peers and adults in giving useful feedback to a student about his/her work.

Evaluating a Learning Portfolio

Checklists

A checklist provides a list of essential criteria. This may include things that should be in the portfolio, and well as some criteria for how the collection is organized. When evaluating the portfolio, criteria are marked as being complete/met or not.

This portfolio has...

❏ Title page
❏ Table of contents
❏ Minimum of 6 artifacts
❏ All pages firmly attached
❏ A reflection for each artifact

Rating Scales

A rating scale provides a little more structure. The criteria are listed, and there is a range or a scale that represents the degree of success. Many rating scales are five-point scales with 1 being a low degree of success and 5 being high. Each criteria is then considered and a score between 1 and 5 assigned.

Well organized	1	2	3	4	5
Neat	1	2	3	4	5
Includes a range/diversity of artifacts	1	2	3	4	5
Evidence of reflection	1	2	3	4	5
Evidence of learning	1	2	3	4	5
Link to major concepts	1	2	3	4	5

Rubrics

See Rubric for Portfolio Assessment (page 119).

A rubric allows for the greatest amount of support and direction. Any rubric is most effective when created by or with the students in advance. When students clearly understand the expectations upon them, they are better able to work towards achieving success. When they are not sure what is expected, they spend a lot of time roaming around in the unknown, not sure what to do. For some, this confusion can lead to giving up rather than trying to figure out the expectations. Four easy steps will help you construct a rubric to use with students' learning portfolios.

1. Decide on the criteria. What are the areas that will be evaluated?
2. Decide on the range of levels. Will this be a four-, five-, or six-point rubric?
3. Describe what each of the criteria "looks like" at each of the levels.
4. Review the rubric. Is it fair? Does it represent your expectations?

Promoting Positive Writing

Providing feedback involves more than just assessing students' work. Effective feedback also involves providing students with useful information about the task in general in an effort to help them be more successful. Helping students to see the targets that we set for them, assisting them in understanding what effective writing looks like, and showing them how they can create pieces of writing that they are proud of is no small task. What teachers can do, however, is to deliberately try a few things. Below are 10 ways that teachers can help students to improve their writing.

1. Share many strong models.
2. Create a chart with the expectations listed: "_____ looks like this." Post this in your classroom.
3. Show students three or four samples that range from poor to excellent. Ask them to examine the differences.
4. Build a rubric that identifies expectations and provides descriptors for three to five levels of success.
5. Give students a copy of a writing sample and a checklist to keep in their notebook.
6. Complete a writing sample together as a class.
7. Provide clear and specific feedback to students about their work. Tell them exactly what they did well and what needs to be improved (e.g., "The information presented on your poster is accurate and appropriate. You could improve its effectiveness by using subheadings in a larger font to help guide the reader.")
8. Show students how to use graphic organizers to provide the framework and organization required for future writing.
9. Have students work together to complete a text or to provide specific feedback to each other.
10. Don't expect all writing to be made public and perfect. Always consider your audience and purpose.

Appendices

Possibilities List

Possibilities List

Basic Web

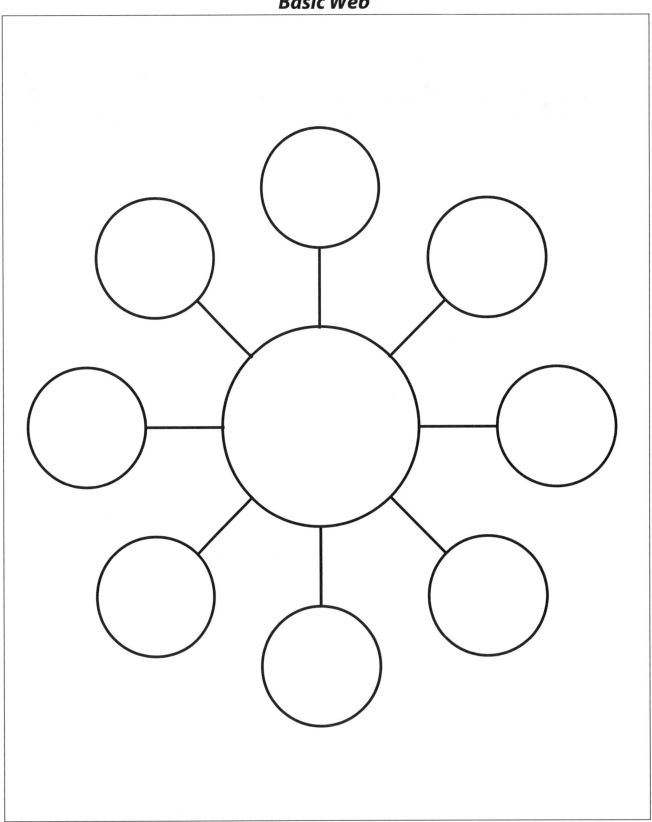

Cluster Web

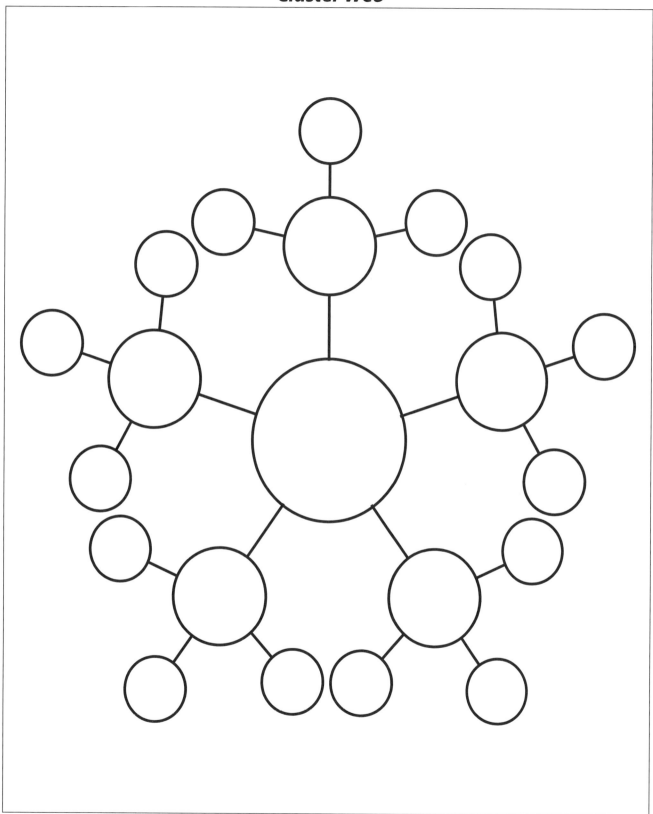

Venn Diagrams

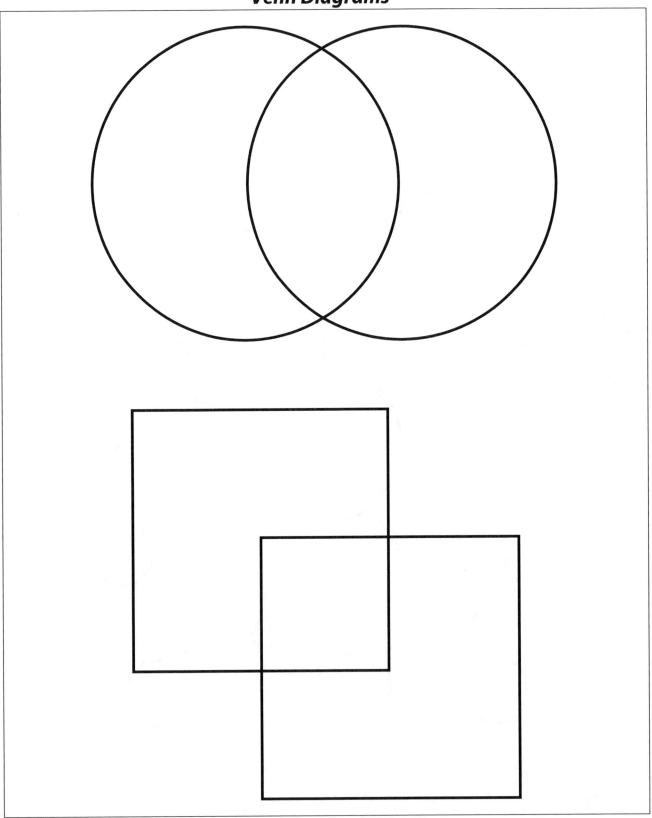

Flow Chart

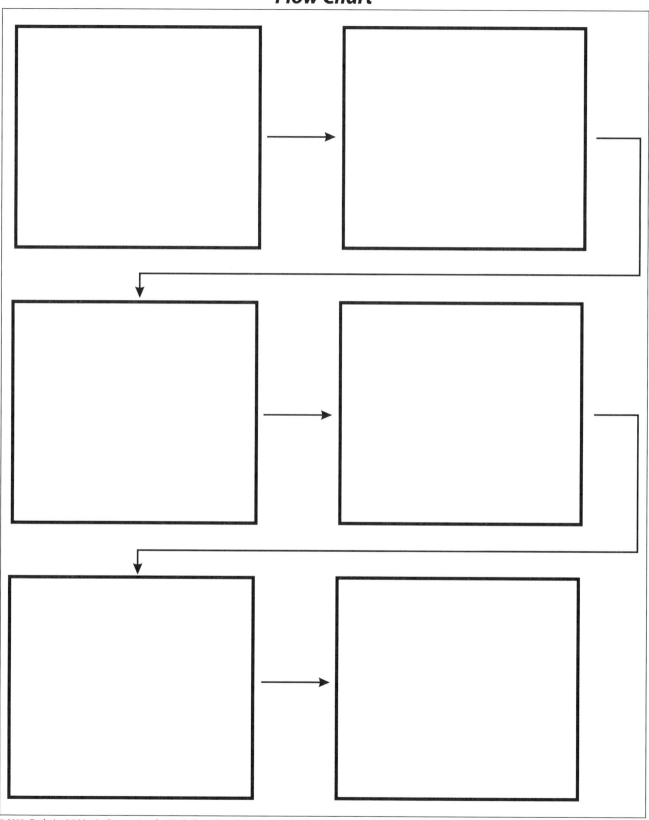

Note-Making Chart

| Name: |
| Date: |
| Course: |

| Topic: |
| Sources: |

Key Vocabulary	Important Information	Summary Sentence(s)
Visual		Questions

Note-Making List

1) _____

    a) _____

        i) _____

        ii) _____

    b) _____

        i) _____

        ii) _____

2) _____

    a) _____

        i) _____

        ii) _____

    b) _____

        i) _____

        ii) _____

What/Did/But/Result

Topic:			
What	**Did**	**But**	**Result**

Summary Sentence

Top-Ten Spelling Strategies

1. Give It a Go: Try writing the word several ways; which looks right?

2. Guess and Check: Write it and then check another source to see if you are right.

3. Picture the Word: Picture it in your head, write it, and ask yourself if it looks right.

4. Think of Words that Sound the Same: Think of other words that have a similar sound and try using the same pattern.

5. Break It Up: Spell the parts of the word you do know—smaller words, root words, prefixes (beginnings), or suffixes (endings) (e.g., *government* has the word *govern* in it).

6. Think of Word Origins: Latin and Greek origins of words can help to explain its meaning and establish a pattern for spelling (e.g., aquaculture, pentagon, octagon).

7. Use a Mnemonic Device: Learn a technique for remembering the correct spelling of a word.

8. Ask Someone: Get help from another student, a teacher, a parent, etc.

9. Use the Dictionary or Check Another Source: Look for the word in a textbook, poster, etc.

10. Choose a Different Word: Do this only if the other word is just as appropriate in communicating your message

Basic Punctuation

Punctuation	Symbol	Use	Example
period	.	• end punctuation • signals a statement, information	Rainforests are home to many species of plants and animals.
question mark	?	• end punctuation • signals a question, asking something	Do you agree that smoking is unhealthy?
exclamation mark	!	• end punctuation • signals emotion	I love math!
comma	,	• indicates to the reader the need to pause • separates parts of a sentence (e.g., in a list, in a date or address, phrases that interrupt a sentence)	Tom used a calculator, graph paper, ruler, and pencil to complete the problem. Martin Luther King Jr. was assassinated on April 4, 1968. Fluids, such as water and corn syrup, are substances that flow.
colon	:	• indicates more information is to follow (e.g., a list, a subtitle)	Define the following angles: acute, right, obtuse, straight, reflex. Jane was reading the book, *Anorexia Nervosa: A Deadly Disorder*.
semi colon	;	• connects two related sentences instead of using a conjunction	Water is a powerful force; it can destroy entire regions.
quotation mark	" "	• used to indicate dialogue/conversation • indicates a direct quote from another source	Einstein said, "The most beautiful experience we can have is the mysterious."
apostrophe	'	• shows possession • indicates the word is a contraction (two words combined with the apostrophe replacing the missing letters)	Newton's inventions have changed the world. Don't underestimate the power of peer pressure.
parentheses	( )	• adds information that you don't need or want as part of the main sentence • directs the reader to a new location for additional information • suggests pronunciation	Tsunamis (formerly called tidal waves) are some of the largest, most devastating waves known. Population growth between the 1840s and the 1860s was dramatic (figure 2). A convex (kon-veks') lens is curved like the outside of a ball.

Visual Options

Visual	Purpose	Component	Example
Photo			
Illustration			
Diagram			
Cross section or Cut-away			
Chart			
Timeline			
Table			
Bar graph			
Line graph			
Pie graph			
Scatter plot			
Map			

Descriptive Writing

Framework	Examples	Keywords
• Begins with a general statement that identifies the topic • Ideas are described in such a way that the reader can envision the topic. • Language appeals to the five senses and helps to paint the picture.	observations examples connections comments questions predictions	sensory words

Informational Writing

Framework	Examples	Keywords
• Begins with a general statement that identifies the topic • Each paragraph describes one of the subtopics. • Ideas are presented factually. • Language is neutral and impersonal.	reports essays	technical terms

Persuasive Writing

Framework	Examples	Keywords
• Begins by stating the topic and position • Ideas or opinions are then supported with evidence or a convincing argument. • Often includes statistics, reasoning, and use of emotional or strong language • May include possible counter arguments and the rationale for their ineffectiveness • Concludes by reiterating the initial argument and position	letters to the editor proposals judgments or arguments advertisements résumés	*must* *essential*

Procedural/Sequential Writing

Framework	Examples	Keywords
• Begins with a goal or purpose • Is sequential or linear in nature, explaining the steps or process involved • Each step or part of the process is easily identified and clearly explains the event or task.	timelines directions/instructions lab reports	*first* *next* *following* *finally*

Comparative Writing

Framework	Examples	Keywords
• Begins by identifying the items to be compared and possibly the criteria for comparison • Describes the qualities or characteristics of the individual items, and explains their similarities and differences	consumer reports metaphors analogies	*unlike* *just as* *more* *most* words ending in *-er*

Personal Writing

Framework	Examples	Keywords
• Begins with the date and topic • Proceeds to describe the topic, event, or idea from a personal point of view • May include likes and dislikes, opinions, suggestions. • Opinions should be supported with a rational and evidence. • May include visual forms of representation such as sketches, charts etc.	diaries journals self-assessments logs reflections on learning opinion pieces	*I think...* *I believe...* *I learned...* *I wonder...* *This reminds me of..*

List–Group–Label

List			
Label			
Group			

Writing Matrix

1	2	3	4
	6	7	8
	10	11	12
	14	15	16
5	9	13	17

Argument–Evidence–Source

Argument	Evidence	Source

Hitting the Target

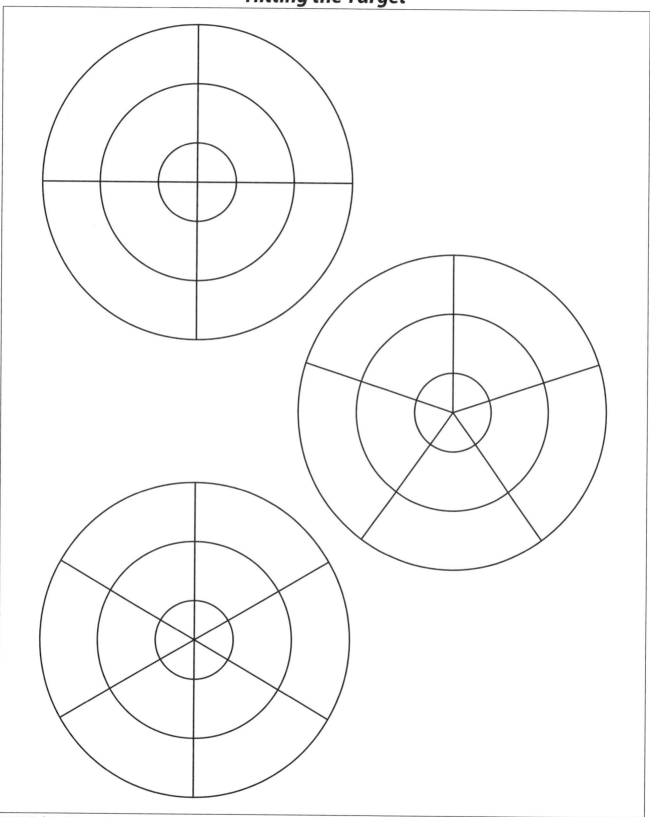

Putting It all Together

Alternatives to using "then... then... then..."	
How to _____ 1. 2. 3. 4. 5. 6. 7. 8.	

Components of a Lab Report

		Purpose or Explanation	Key Words
Question	Question	What are you trying to find out. • the variables or relationships that will be investigated	*why, what, how*
	Hypothesis	What you think will happen. • forecasts how one variable will affect a second variable • proposes a logical explanation that can be tested	*if...then*
Procedure	Materials Needed	A list of equipment and materials used	quantity and amounts (mass, volume, length)
	Variables Controlled	Manipulated variable • a factor or condition that is intentionally changed; also known as independent variable Responding variable • a factor or condition that might be affected as a result of the change; also known as the dependent variable Controlled Variable • a variable that is not changed in an effort to limit sources of error	*changed, increased, decreased, increments* *affected, increased, decreased* *compared, same, continue*
	Steps	A step-by-step process for completing the experiment	*First, second, third*, etc. *finally, following, next*
Results	Observations	What was observed • Qualitative observations describe. • Quantitative observations measure.	words that describe size, quantity, shape, color, smell, location, movement
	Data and Results	Includes data tables, graphs, diagrams, etc.	
	Analysis	Interpretation or findings from data	*appears, is, was*
Conclusion	Explanation	Factual summary of what happened	*therefore, in conclusion*

Plus/Minus

+	—

Pro/Con

Option	PRO	Pts.	CON	Pts.

Point and Counterpoint

Focus Question:

Position:

Point	Counterpoint

New–Now–Next Journal

	New	Now	Next
week 1			
week 2			
week 3			
week 4			

Me & You Journal

date	Me	You

4-Square Log

Key Words	Ideas and New Information
Picture or Visual	**Questions I Still Have**

Poster Presentation Points

Organization

- Move from left to right, top to bottom.

- Place the main idea in the centre.

- Create a pattern that is easy for the eye to follow.

Space

- Use all of the space—don't cram.

- Balance the borders and white space.

- Space the print so it is easy to read.

Size

- Size is important—can you read the poster from a distance?

- Greater importance requires greater size (e.g., headings vs subheadings).

- Use a larger size to make things stand out.

Color

- Choose colors that are associated with your topic.

- Use color in borders, visuals, and words.

- Have a reason for every color you use.

- Sometimes less is more; too much color can be distracting.

Visuals

- Include symbols, charts, graphs, maps, photos, diagrams, tables, illustrations, etc.

- Use visuals to communicate ideas instead of the print.

- Use visuals to add meaning to the print.

- Clarity is key.

WWE

Poster:			
	W What?	W Why?	E Effectiveness?
Purpose			
Essential and effective information			
Organization			
Space			
Size			
Color			
Visuals			

Here to There

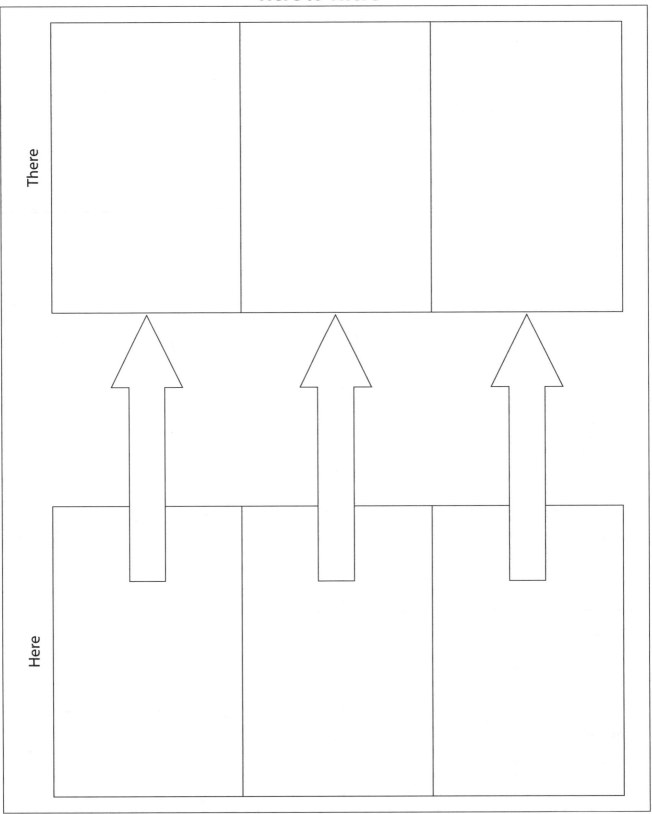

Appendix M: Profile for Nonfiction Writing

Checklist Template

Checklist for _____	Checklist for _____
❏ _____	❏ _____
❏ _____	❏ _____
❏ _____	❏ _____
❏ _____	❏ _____
❏ _____	❏ _____
❏ _____	❏ _____
❏ _____	❏ _____
❏ _____	❏ _____
❏ _____	❏ _____
❏ _____	❏ _____
❏ _____	❏ _____
❏ _____	❏ _____
❏ _____	❏ _____
❏ _____	❏ _____
❏ _____	❏ _____
❏ _____	❏ _____
❏ _____	❏ _____
❏ _____	❏ _____
❏ _____	❏ _____
❏ _____	❏ _____

Checklist for Informational Writing

Re-read your informational report and check off the criteria that you have met:

❑ Begins with a general statement that identifies the topic.

❑ Each paragraph describes one of the subtopics.

❑ Ideas are presented factually.

❑ Language is neutral and impersonal.

❑ Ends with a conclusion that summarizes the topic.

❑ Spelling is conventional.

❑ Punctuation is used correctly.

❑ Writing is easy to read.

❑ Information presented is accurate.

❑ Sources are cited.

❑ Accomplishes the purpose of the assignment.

❑ _____

❑ _____

❑ _____

❑ _____

❑ _____

❑ _____

Checklist for Persuasive Writing

Re-read your persuasive writing and check off the criteria that you have met:

❑ Begins by stating the topic and position.

❑ Ideas or opinions are then supported with evidence or a convincing argument.

❑ Often includes statistics and reasoning.

❑ May include possible counter-arguments and the rationale for their ineffectiveness.

❑ Powerful and emotional language is used.

❑ Concludes by reiterating the initial argument and position.

❑ Spelling is conventional.

❑ Punctuation is used correctly.

❑ Writing is easy to read.

❑ Information presented is accurate.

❑ Sources are cited.

❑ Accomplishes the purpose of the assignment.

❑ _____

❑ _____

❑ _____

❑ _____

❑ _____

❑ _____

Checklist for Procedural Writing

Re-read your procedural writing and check off the criteria that you have met:

❏ Begins with a goal or purpose.

❏ Is sequential or linear in nature, explaining the steps or process involved.

❏ Each step or part of the process is easily identified and clearly explains the event or task.

❏ Sequential language is used (*first*, *next*, *finally*, etc.).

❏ A numbered list is used.

❏ May include a diagram or flow chart to support explanation.

❏ Spelling is conventional.

❏ Punctuation is used correctly.

❏ Writing is easy to read.

❏ Information presented is accurate.

❏ Accomplishes the purpose of the assignment.

❏ _____

❏ _____

❏ _____

❏ _____

❏ _____

❏ _____

Checklist for Comparative Writing

Re-read your comparative writing and check off the criteria that you have met:

❏ Begins by identifying the items to be compared, and possibly the criteria for comparison.

❏ Describes the qualities or characteristics of the individual items, and explains their similarities and differences.

❏ Ends with a conclusion that restates the comparison.

❏ Uses comparative language (*similarly*, *rather than*, *unlike*, etc.).

❏ Spelling is conventional.

❏ Punctuation is used correctly.

❏ Writing is easy to read.

❏ Information presented is accurate.

❏ Sources are cited.

❏ Accomplishes the purpose of the assignment.

❏ _____

❏ _____

❏ _____

❏ _____

❏ _____

❏ _____

Sample Rubric

	1	2	3	4
Organization • sequence • focus • cohesion	• Unclear or difficult to follow.	• Lacks a clear introduction therefore the purpose is unclear. • Organization is not clear and paragraphing is weak. • Sequence of ideas needs work.	• Purpose is evident and efforts are made to organize the writing accordingly. • Transitions between paragraphs is attempted but may lack effectiveness or creativity.	• Structure suits and achieves the purpose. • Writing has a clear organization. • There is effective flow from one paragraph to the next.
Ideas • accurate • detailed	• Many factual errors. • Writing is vague and not complete.	• Some inconsistencies. • Lacks the necessary detail.	• Information is accurate. • More details may be required in order to support the main ideas.	• All information is accurate. • Level of detail effectively supports the main ideas.
Engagement • voice • word choice • variety • creativity	• Writing lacks interest and engagement. • Does not sound like an original piece of work.	• Voice needs to be added to the writing. • More creativity and careful selection of word choice would improve the piece.	• Writing is effective in capturing the reader's attention.	• Writing is creative and uses interesting and effective choice of words. • Captures the reader's attention and won't let go.
Conventions • spelling • punctuation • grammar • sentence structure	• Errors in spelling, punctuation, and grammar are distracting or make reading difficult. • Incomplete or ineffective sentence structure.	• Editing is still required. • There are errors in some basic spelling, punctuation, and grammar. • There is little variation in sentence structure.	• Basic spelling, punctuation, and grammar are correct. • A variety of is sentences used.	• Very few or minor errors in spelling, punctuation, and grammar. • Sophisticated sentence structure is used.
Visual Supports • charts • diagrams • maps • photos	• Includes no visuals.	• Visuals are included but provide minimal detail or support.	• Visuals are used to support the text but may not extend the meaning of the text.	• Detailed visuals are appropriately placed and help to support and extend the meaning of the text.

Editors' Marks

¶ or par	new paragraph
∧	insert (i.e. more information)
ℐ	delete
om	omitted word
sp	spelling error
p	punctuation error
≡	capital letter (triple underline)
/	lower case
var	lack in variety in sentence structure
w	wordy
awk	awkward
#	insert space
⌒	close up space
num	error in use of numbers

PentaRep Template

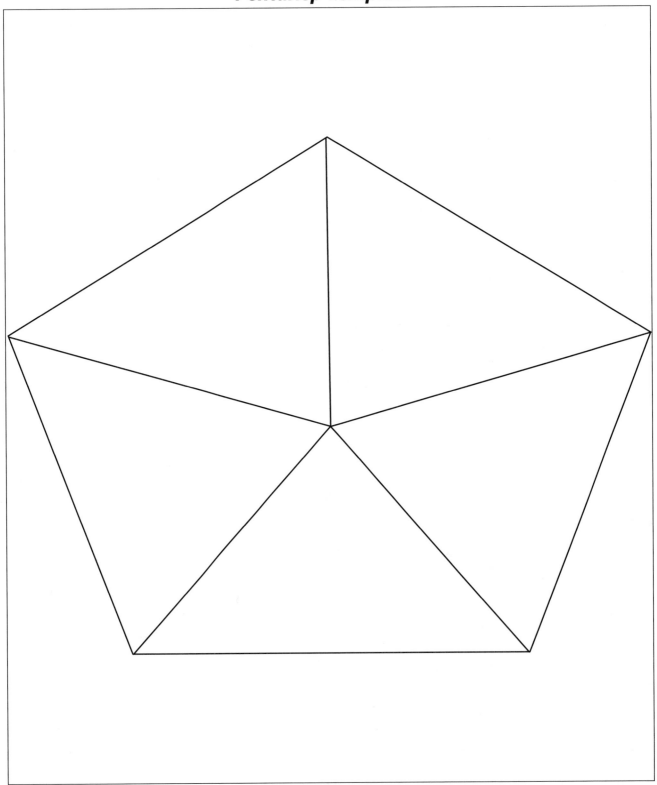

Student Reflection Prompt Cards

• This is an example of my best work because…	• This is something that I had to work especially hard on…	• This was something I found especially difficult…
• This is not my best work. Next time I would like to…	• These two piece of work show growth and improvement. The first piece…. • The second piece…	• The thing about my work that I want you to notice is…
• If I could change something about this piece of work I would…	• The thing I found most difficult was…	• When doing this work I learned…

Audience Feedback Prompts

Something I noticed is …	The thing that impressed me most was…
A question I have is …	A suggestion I would make is…

Rubric for Portfolio Assessment

Name: _____ Course: _____ Date: _____

	1	2	3	4
Organization and neatness	• Portfolio is disorganized and lacks basic neatness.	• Portfolio is organized • Work is securely attached.	• Portfolio is well organized and is neatly attached in the correct place. • Basic neatness is evident but creativity is lacking.	• The portfolio has a logical organized structure. • All work is securely attached in the correct place. • Work is neat and demonstrates creativity.
Diversity	• No or minimal artifacts have been included.	• Artifacts included are similar.	• A variety of artifacts have been included.	• Artifacts represent a complete picture of the student as a learner within this course.
Depth of understanding	• Minimal understanding is evident.	• Some evidence of understanding is evident. • Gaps are apparent.	• Artifacts demonstrate understanding of key concepts and key processes.	• The range of artifacts selected shows a deep understanding of the course and the required concepts and processes.
Reflection on learning	• No or minimal reflection.	• Some artifacts have a reflection. • Reflections are basic and deal with surface-level issues (neatness, length, organization).	• All artifacts have a reflection attached. • An attempt has been made to include thoughtful reflections.	• All artifacts have a refection attached. • Reflections show a depth of understanding of the concepts and of the learner and the learning process.
Feedback from others	• No evidence of sharing with others.	• Includes feedback from one person.	• Includes feedback from two or more people.	• Includes feedback from two or more people. • Shows evidence that feedback has been incorporated into future learning.

Index